NAMING THE DEAD

'Maya Evans cares and stands up to show it. This brings
the change the world cries for. Inspiring! Thank you.'

Brian Haw

NAMING THE DEAD
A Serious Crime

Maya Anne Evans
with Milan Rai

JNV Publications

Published by JNV Publications, Autumn 2006.
An imprint of Drava Papers.

JNV Publications, 29 Gensing Road, St Leonards on Sea
East Sussex TN38 0HE
Telephone: 01424 428 792   Email: info@j-n-v.org

www.j-n-v.org

ISBN 978-1-904527-10-7

Typeset in Gill and Garamond by JNV Publications.

Printed by Footprint Workers Co-op.
'Footprint is a printing company operating from the cellar of
Cornerstone Housing Co-op in Leeds. Footprint was set up to
provide as eco-friendly and ethical a printing service as possible
and to provide flexible and ethical employment for political
activists. We are members of Radical Routes, the network of
co-ops working for radical social change.'
www.footprinters.co.uk

For Sarah, Myvanwy and Emily

Contents

Acknowledgements

Thank you to Milan Rai who encouraged me to seriously consider writing this book, who has shown patience and humour throughout. Whose skill, judgment and talent has enabled this to happen.

Thanks also to Emily Johns who has taught and nurtured me so much through the years. My role model of a strong woman, without whom nothing.

A special thanks to Arkady Johns and Patrick Nicholson for their support.

Susan Johns, Cedric Knight, John Rety, David Polden, Heather Seddon, Roy Hiscock and Pauline Rowe, Andrea Needham, Judy Dewsbury have all enabled this to happen.

Emma Sangster for her tireless work in the peace movement and the anti-SOCPA campaign.

John Enefer for his encouragement and ideas.

Joanne Hanlon, Raquel Ajates Gonzalez, Jenny Allan, Nicola Palmer and Jon Levi for their humour and support.

Jonathan Stevenson and Gabriel Carlyle for their wise advice and contributions. Esme Needham for smiles and hugs.

Louie White Dyer for cakes. Billy, Leigh, Chris, Rosie and Simon, you are all appreciated.

Author's Note

The source for the dialogue used in this book is primarily my own memory. Much dialogue around the trial has been taken from police notes and newspaper reports. The dialogue from Newsnight and the Today Programme has been transcribed.

This book is based on interviews of me by Mil, talking about my memories of events. Mil then transcribed the interviews and merged them with my written accounts of the same events, with rigorous re-editing. Through the writing we managed to get details, and through the interviews we managed to get feelings.

Many names of childhood friends have been changed in order to protect their identities around sensitive issues.

Chapter 1

Arrested

25 October 2005

A third of the way down Whitehall, Mil suddenly emerges from the crowd ahead of us, looks me in the eye, and says calmly: 'The police came over and spoke to me just now. We will definitely be arrested if we go ahead. They said it is "zero tolerance".' I'm shocked. I've been hoping we won't be arrested. Until now, I thought it was a 60 per cent chance that we'd be arrested—just for reading the names of people who'd died in the Iraq War. The tourists pass around us on the pavement, wandering down from Trafalgar Square towards the Houses of Parliament. Mil asks: 'Do you really want to do this? You can change your mind right now.' For a moment, it flashes through my mind that I *can* wriggle out of this, I don't *have to* go through with it. I've never been arrested before (I was detained once for a few hours in Belgium). I hate personal confrontations of any kind, and the idea of a face-to-face conflict with the ultimate authority figure, a police officer, is really uncomfortable. Do I really want to be arrested and prosecuted, and end up with a criminal record, and with a £1,000 fine? For half a second, I don't want to go any further.

I haven't been entirely focused until now. We'd met earlier on the steps of St Martin-in-the-Fields, on the corner of Trafalgar Square. It was overcast and there was a light drizzle. I'd arrived late, feeling flustered, and anxious about the possibility of being arrested. My friend Adesina, who I've known from school, had come along to support me. After we turned up, Mil had gone on ahead to meet our friend Cedric Knight, one of our legal observers. After handing over my phone and other personal items to Gabriel Carlyle, another observer, I'd gone looking for Mil, carrying our large cardboard signs, still very worried.

After that flash of doubt and fear, I felt myself becoming hyper-aware. Everything was brighter and louder. I was suddenly very calm. I said to Mil, and to myself, 'I'm ready to do this'. I could feel myself putting on this façade of being a confident, strong person who knew what she was doing. I had to put my weaknesses and my personal feelings away. There was something important I had to do, and I needed to be very focused.

I'd mentally prepared myself for this the day before, and, after that half-second of wanting to run away, I felt ready for everything that was about to happen. It was very important to me to carry out this remembrance ceremony, and to remind people about the tragedy of the war in Iraq, and all the people who have died there.

Our protest was part of an international ceremony of remembrance we'd helped to initiate, called '100,000 Rings for the people of Iraq'. We were helping to mark the first anniversary of the publication of a landmark paper in *The Lancet*, the world's most respected medical journal. This was explained on the four-foot-high cardboard signs we were carrying towards Downing Street. One said:

> '100,000 Rings for Iraq. A year ago, a study in the medical journal *The Lancet* estimated that 100,000 Iraqis had died of war-related causes since the invasion of Iraq.'

The other said:

> 'Remembering the 100,000 Iraqis and 96 British soldiers who have died in this war. An international ceremony of remembrance and resistance.'

(Unfortunately, a British soldier had died since the sign had been made a few days earlier, making it incorrect.) Our event was one of dozens being held around the US and Western Europe. The US group Voices for Creative Non-Violence (VCNV) aimed to inspire 100 communities to each ring a bell 1,000 times, to mark the death toll estimated by the *Lancet* team. VNCV had asked 'Justice Not Vengeance' (JNV), the small British peace group Mil and I co-ordinate, to be co-initiators of 100,000 Rings.

Mil (Milan Rai) and I decided to carry out our 1,000 minute ceremony in four parts. During each part, we would ring a bell once a minute. After each ring we would read the name of an Iraqi civilian who had died during the invasion or occupation, and the name of a British soldier who had died in the war. The first ceremony was held in Brighton in a peace park, and the second ceremony was held in North London, at the military base in Northwood, Herts. In Brighton, we'd been on our own. At Northwood, we'd been joined by two Muslim friends: Sonia, the convenor of 'Children Against War', and her mother Saeeda.

I don't remember actually walking down the rest of Whitehall. I just remember getting to the crowd barriers and attaching our cardboard signs, facing Downing Street. The white Cenotaph, which remembers all the British soldiers who have died in war, was to our left. To our right was the new black memorial to the Women of World War II. Behind us was the Ministry of Defence, and directly in front of us were the gates of Downing Street. I'd given my Tibetan bell to Adesina for safekeeping, as we thought we wouldn't get a chance to use it, and we didn't want it to be confiscated by the police for nothing. We were just going to read the names of the dead.

I took the list of British soldiers, while Mil took the much longer list of Iraqi civilians who had died in the conflict. As we got ready to read the names, the police spilled across the road. I was approached by a stocky, grim police officer who I now know to be Police Constable Paul

McInally. He was unsympathetic. Mil and I were warned that we were breaching the Serious Organised Crime and Police Act by holding an unauthorized demonstration. We were each given a map of the 'restricted area' around Parliament where unauthorized demonstrations are not permitted. Mil asked them whether they were aware that 100,000 people had died in Iraq because of the war. The police gave us five minutes to leave.

I said very little to the police. I concentrated on reading out the names of the British dead. I read each soldier's name, his rank, and his age. Meanwhile, Mil was reading out the names of Iraqi civilians who've died violently as a result of the invasion and occupation.

Whenever you read out the list of names, a shiver goes through you, and you feel sad for the people who've died. You feel so sad that they have lost their lives in such an unnecessary war. The list of Iraqi civilian names was published by Iraq Body Count, which keeps track of all reported violent deaths in Iraq. Their list contains information about people's occupations, where they died, and the manner of their death. Previously, we'd confronted all this heart-breaking information for four hours at a time. I'd felt close to the people whose passing we were acknowledging. Somehow, now, reading the names in the presence of the police made the whole experience much more intense. And I felt almost as if the police were being affected by the reading more than I was. I had to be disciplined and focused, and to remain polite and calm at all times. How I behaved would reflect on our ceremony.

While we were reading the names, and waiting for the police to arrest us, I saw my friend Adesina directly outside Downing Street, pointing a video camera towards us. She was approached by, and then surrounded by, a group of police officers. I felt really bad because I had asked her to video our event, and now it had led to her being harassed by the police. I could see from her hand gestures and body language that it was quite a difficult experience for her, and I felt really torn. Then I saw them starting to search her bag—under section 44 of the Terrorism Act 2000, I later discovered. Part of me wanted to dash across the road to support her. The other part of me realized that I'd probably just make her problems even worse.

Despite the fact that we knew we were about to be arrested at any moment, I was more concerned about Adesina than about myself. I'd had time to prepare myself mentally for the experience, and I knew what the process ahead was like. Adesina hadn't had any preparation at all, and she didn't have any idea what could happen to her.

Slowly, however, the situation seemed to calm down.

I still felt angry and powerless. Our friend Cedric, who is a tall blond Englishman, was also taking pictures—on our side of the road—and he wasn't being harassed at all. A professional photographer, Molly Cooper, had arrived and she was also being allowed to photograph us freely. I felt as though the police were going for the easy target, a lone African Muslim woman wearing a headscarf.

Finally, after a quarter of an hour, the police arrested us. Mil was the first to be led into an unmarked police van. I should explain that at this point Mil's arrest seemed to everyone involved much more serious than mine. I was just another person being arrested for 'participating' in an unauthorized demonstration under the Serious Organized Crime and Police Act (SOCPA). People had been getting arrested for this since 1 August 2005, when SOCPA came into force. But Mil was the first person to be arrested for 'organizing' an unauthorized demonstration. He had *notified* the police about our demonstration, but he'd refused to ask for *permission* to hold it. He therefore faced a much higher maximum penalty than me, possibly months in prison.

So on 25 October, it was Mil's arrest which we all thought might possibly get some media attention. That's why, for example, the short video made of our arrest by Rikki, an Indymedia activist, focuses almost entirely on Mil. (You can see it at http://tinyurl.com/omwho .)

When I decided to take part in the demonstration and risk arrest, no one—least of all me—imagined that the end result could be mainstream media attention. I thought it was possible I might be interviewed once or maybe twice as a result, perhaps for the *Hastings Observer*. I thought maybe *Peace News* would feature it. (*Peace News* did cover the story—I wrote the article!)

From what I'd seen, most of the time when people carry out nonviolent civil disobedience, it isn't reported at all in the national newspapers. If it is mentioned, it's a small item in the 'news in brief' column buried inside the paper. That suited me fine. It may seem funny now, with the way things turned out, but I didn't want the pressure of being in the spotlight. I hate public speaking. Even now, after all media work I've done in the last year, I avoid public speaking. The other day I was invited to speak at a public meeting alongside an MP, in a hall that seats 100 people. I felt physically sick at the prospect.

When I was arrested by PC McInally, I still felt strangely calm and focused. I know that being arrested for the first time can be an emotional experience for a lot of people, but after all the preparation I'd been through, and my moment of clarity earlier, it all just felt like a very natural progression. The most important thing was that I just could not believe that what we were doing was wrong. I didn't see how reading the names of the dead without the permission of the police could be wrong—morally or legally. I did feel resentful towards the authorities for making a law that meant we could be arrested for carrying out a peaceful protest of remembering the dead, and I felt more resentful towards the police officers for allowing themselves to go along with this law, but overall I felt calm.

As we pulled away from the curb, I saw Adesina leaving the scene, probably on her way to the V&A Museum. I could relax about her, but what about myself? How would I cope with being in the hands of the police?

Chapter 2

Laburnum Street

1979-1998

I was born in a council flat on Laburnum Street in Hackney, in London, on 18 December 1979. I spent my childhood in that flat, and my Mum still lives there now. Laburnum Street had three laburnum trees on it, all standing in front of my block of flats. The trees are the best thing about the street, especially when they're in flower, with their startling yellow flowers. Whenever I see laburnum trees, I feel at home. Starlings roosted in the trees, and they would start a huge racket as the day dawned.

I was born in the small back bedroom in our flat, which is the bedroom I had when I was growing up. I do have this wacky 'earliest memory', which I might have dreamt or imagined, which is an aerial view of my mum, in bed, and my sister's outside the door, and my step-grandmother's there (I know she was there from stories that I've been told), and she's beckoning my sister to come away, and that the baby is coming. That's probably an imagined memory of my birth.

My early memories are of my sister. Her real name is Myvanwy, but I always called her Miffy. I adored my sister intensely as a child. She taught me how to read the time, and how to tie my laces, and that our mum's name was 'Sarah'. As a teenager, she taught me the words of Prince songs, and how to cook scrambled egg on toast.

My father wasn't around when I was growing up. Miffy's dad, who was different to my dad, wasn't around either, but every few months we did visit him in Seven Sisters in north London. I enjoyed those visits. He was Afro-Caribbean, and he'd have these gambling circles of all his other Caribbean friends, and they'd all sit around playing dominoes or poker. One of his friends really liked me and used to slip me what seemed like lots of money (it was probably pennies). The thing I remember most was that Miffy's dad had a fridge in his front room, and he always gave us really cold glasses of Coca-Cola with ice. So it was: 'Wow! We're going to my sister's dad's!'

My Mum once told me that before I was born my father had told her the baby was going to be a girl. He didn't want responsibility for me, but he still wanted to give me my name. He said that 'Maya' was a ghost of fire which haunts a house and draws people in. He told my Mum that I would always be a ghost haunting him and drawing him back to England. This hasn't turned out to be true—so far. Absent fathers were the norm in Hackney. It was only later in life I realized how much of a hole that leaves.

Almost the only clear memory I have of my father is the last time I saw him. I was four or five, and someone knocked on the door. I asked who it was, and he said 'Aloke'. I let him in. It was quite early in the morning because the curtains were still drawn in the front room. I said that my mum was upstairs in the bath, and that she'd be a few minutes and then come down. We didn't really say anything to each other after that. He stood there. Then he got an envelope out of his pocket, and he placed it on the mantelpiece, and then he left. My Mum came down, and she opened the envelope, and there was about £50 in it. She started crying and she said: 'That's it. That's the last time we'll see your dad. He's gone back to India.'

My Mum is possibly the strongest woman I know. She's both physically and mentally strong. Some of my favourite childhood memories are of the holidays Mum took us on.

Mum loves walking in the countryside and bird-watching. She'd take me and my sister hiking in the Peak District, or along the Pembrokeshire coastline. She'd pack enough supplies for the three of us for a fortnight, and carry it all on her back. Youth Hostel wardens would greet us with amazement when we turned up bedraggled after walking all day in the rain with heavy packs. As city kids Miffy and I resented having to walk long distances in the rain. Now I look back on these holidays with great fondness.

When I was growing up, our part of Hackney was mostly white working class and black Afro-Caribbean, and in its own way quite conventional. There were very few Asian people in my primary school. There were five Vietnamese people in the whole school, and one of them, Huong Lan, was my best friend throughout primary school. I experienced a lot of Vietnamese cooking at her house. They ate a lot of noodles and rice-based dishes, which I enjoyed. So primary school was roughly 50 per cent white, 45 per cent Afro-Caribbean, and 5 per cent other. Now it's much more multicultural, but at the time Miffy and I were unusual. We were sisters, and she's half-black and I'm half-Indian, and my mum was a single parent. You could sense the whispers as we were walking out of school together.

Now it's gentrified and there's been a lot of building, but then the area was very run-down. Back then, on the corner of Laburnum Street and Kingsland Road, where there's now the big Suleymaniye Mosque, it was just waste ground where you could see large rats running around in the rubbish. On the other hand, we were on the top floor of our block, and we could just see Regent's Canal through the trees. Nearby was the disused Shoreditch Library, which was a run-down building with grilles covering the windows and rats running around in the basement. (You could hear them from the bus stop.) Now it's an immaculate, pristine white block of high-class flats.

Where there's now a new council estate on Laburnum Street, there used to be the remains of a gasworks, and you could still smell gas as you passed by on the street. Despite all that, there was a strong sense of community. People would look after each other. You could go out and play on the streets, and go to friends' houses, and there was a sense that people would keep an eye on each other's kids. At the same time, it was a rough area. There was a lot of crime; you'd see violence on the streets all the time. You had to become street-wise and learn to spot trouble. You learned how to look after yourself.

My sister left when she was 15, and I was 11. It was after half a year of my Mum and my sister fighting non-stop. She went to live with a friend from school. In a way it was a relief, because all the arguments stopped, though I did miss her. I'd lost my best friend. My sister and my Mum were the volatile ones, I was more of the quiet one. Maybe in the long run that wasn't the best thing for me, because I did end up getting shoved around quite a lot.

I loved secondary school. I could see my friends, and it was an opportunity to learn interesting things sometimes. It didn't have a high standard of exam results, but our head-mistress was proud of the fact that many girls joined the school unable to speak any English and left with at least some GCSEs. I went to Skinners' Company School for Girls in North Hackney, even though I lived in South Hackney. In South Hackney you were either Afro-Caribbean or white. In North Hackney there were more Asian and African people.

White people were the ethnic minority at school. There was only one white person in my class, Nicola. Racism was either between Africans and Caribbean kids or between Sikhs and Muslims. Friendship bonds were very tight and often fights would occur between sets of friends in different schools. Once there was a mini-riot in Stamford Hill because girls from my school had a vendetta with some kids at Tottenham Green School due to an incident at the Hackney festival. I watched from the window of the school library as cars were stopped in the middle of a major cross-roads, and teachers ran about trying to restore order. The police turned up finally, and everyone dispersed.

For myself, I'd rather walk a hundred miles than have an argument with someone. So I would have been useless in a gang, which is probably why I was never in one. I was always very shy and quiet, almost withdrawn. It wasn't until I was 18 that I started to find my feet socially.

There were a lot of Muslim girls at Skinners', and they tended to be quieter, just getting on with their work, and I naturally fell into that fellowship group, going round to their houses and hanging out. Because I'm half-Indian, and a lot of them were Indian and Pakistani, I'd empathize with them and feel comfortable in their culture. I learned how to do lots of Indian cooking from their mums. I remember especially the wonderful cooking of Samina's and Rania's mothers. That's also how I first started being exposed to Islam. There were a lot of Muslim girls because their parents wanted them to go to an all-girls school *and* go to sixth form, and Skinners' was the only non-denominational all-girls school in Hackney with a sixth form. In my class, about 60 per cent of the girls were Muslims. The others were Christians and other religions. Most Muslims were Asian; my friend Adesina was the only Nigerian Muslim in the whole school, I think.

I was about 15 when I first became interested in Islam. One of my good friends, Rania, was very into Islam, and we used to speak at length about it. We were both in the same study class in school, and I opted to do Islam at GCSE, the only non-Muslim in the class. I also went for about a year and a half to one of the Islam study circles she and Adesina went to. It was every Sunday in a private house, in a woman's front room. It was a women-only class, but our teacher, who was amazing, was a man called Ahmed. He knew the whole of the *Qur'an*, and he knew all the *Hadiths*, the stories of the Prophet. He'd go through a chapter, or a few lines, every week and explain what the teachings behind it were. I gained a lot of respect for Islam during this study, and felt very drawn towards it.

Before that, I hadn't had any real religious experiences. Our family are quite atheistic, although Mum did have us christened, because it was 'the thing to do'. Later, she took me and my sister to the local church, St Chad's, a fantastic red-brick building which is still there on the Hackney Road. I remember once whispering to Miffy at church: 'I'm really bored. Where's Mum?' And Miffy whispered back: 'She's gone to the Buddhist Centre.' For about a year, we would go to church while Mum went to the Buddhist Centre round the corner in Bethnal Green.

I stayed on to do A-levels at sixth form. I was continuing to study Islam and thinking about becoming a Muslim. For about two years there was something that was stopping me. I didn't feel right about taking my *shahada* (profession of faith) and becoming a Muslim. I couldn't work out what it was. One day it dawned on me that I just didn't believe that there was only one way. I felt that many religions offered acceptable ways to live your life. Christianity, Islam and other major religions tend to say that they are 'the one true path', and that if you don't follow that path, you're going to go to Hell. I just couldn't accept that, and that held me back from becoming a Muslim.

Despite this, my Muslim teacher Ahmed was the most influential person of my childhood, apart from my family. Although I haven't chosen to follow that path, I empathize a lot with Muslims. In fact, to a great extent I still feel I have many Muslim values, because of what I learned in those study circles. How to conduct yourself, what's fair to other people, morality: much of what I know in these areas is based on what I learned from Ahmed's strand of Islam. I gained a lot in terms of my sense of who I am from those meetings.

Ahmed taught a lot about the ego, and that it was one of the biggest enemies to humankind. He also taught about the equality of women, and its basis in Islam, and that allowed me to see Islam differently. He would say: 'The entrance to Heaven lies at the feet of your mother.'

We rarely discussed politics in the study circle. I don't remember Ahmed expressing his opinions about Palestine or Bosnia or anything like that. But I was aware that a lot of Muslims felt a political dimension to their belief. In year 10, I sat next to a girl called Tahira during maths class, who had the word 'HAMAS' scratched on her calculator. I asked her about it, and she replied with great passion: 'They are freedom fighters who stand up for Muslims. In Palestine, Muslims don't have any weapons, they are being killed in their homes, and nobody cares. In Islam, if one Muslim is suffering then every Muslim is suffering'. Tahira said her older brother was going to join Hamas, and go and fight for Muslims, along with other 'brothers'. Her older brother came one night to a parents' evening, because her parents didn't speak enough English to understand what the teachers were saying. He had a PLO scarf around his neck, and a thick dark beard, and he looked cool. He was at university studying chemistry. I felt huge respect towards him: 'What a passionate person he must be.' In the end, I don't think he ever did go to fight 'jihad'. The last I heard of him, he'd married and settled down in Harrow.

Apart from my Mum and Ahmed, there were other people who had an influence on me, including my cousin Emily Johns, and her partner Mil, who I ended up being arrested with in front of Downing Street. Emily and Mil had a way of life I'd never seen before, with creative and activist lives. They were standing up for what they believed in, involved in the peace movement, and leading lives that didn't involve going to 9 to 5 jobs every day and being ground down by the status quo.

Other influences on me were my great aunts, Aunty Mary and Aunty Meg, who were both very strong, intelligent and independent women. Aunty Meg and my aunt Heather were both revolutionary communists in their earlier years, but I never got to hear much about that. Heather mainly influenced me with her great love of history. She was knowledgeable and enthusiastic about medieval history, which I went on to specialize in at university.

My friends were certain that politics would play some part in my life, because I was very passionate about animal rights issues. I'd always been interested in wildlife: I was in the Young Ornithologists' Club, and when I was a child I adopted a whale. I'd been brought up vegetarian, so from the age of five, I was having to justify my position. This became even more of an issue when I was 10, when Mum and Miffy started eating meat. Mum stopped going to the Buddhist Centre, and she stopped being a vegetarian.

Then I became aware of veganism, and thought to myself: 'If I'm a vegetarian for animal rights reasons, I should go the whole way, because the two industries, the meat industry and the dairy industry, are so intertwined.' Health issues didn't come into it. I still ate chips and samosas!

So I stopped eating dairy products and eggs as well as meat, and even more people started asking me to justify my eating decisions.

My friends would say things like: 'I could really imagine you on a Greenpeace boat with a flag.' At that time, I just couldn't really see it myself. I didn't see how I would get there—from living in South Hackney, not knowing anyone who was involved in that Greenpeace world. People I knew were getting married, or having kids, or going to wild parties. My closest friends were Muslims, mainly interested in religion. Riding on a Greenpeace boat seemed such a wild thing to do, and I was such a level person. I wasn't naughty at school; I was just following the straight path as best I could, and I couldn't imagine anything different.

My ancestors may have been pacifists and union organizers and revolutionaries and animal rights activists, but for myself, I didn't see myself in that world. I would never have imagined back then, for example, that I would end up deliberately risking losing my job by participating in a peaceful protest.

Chapter 3

Suite 14

25 October 2005

As the police van left Whitehall, a woman police officer tried to pump me for information: 'So, are you a student?' Her heart didn't seem to be in it. The van snaked around St Martin-in-the-Fields, where Mil and I had met just an hour earlier, and nosed through the back streets to Charing Cross police station, a huge white building just off the Strand. The van drove through large gates into a courtyard, and the gates closed firmly behind us.

Mil was led off the van, through a metal fence. After a moment, I was told to follow him. Inside, we sat and waited in the 'custody area'. There were benches around the edges of the room, with large whiteboards hanging over some of them detailing who was in which cell, and what their status was. Dominating the room was the custody desk. You stand on one side; the custody sergeant sits on the other (on a platform, so your eyes are on a level).

I didn't feel frightened. I actually felt quite confident. It helped having Mil there, because of his experience with arrest and the police. Mil had talked me through the procedure in advance, so I knew what was about to happen.

I was brought up to the desk. The custody sergeant asked my arresting officer, PC McInally, why I'd been arrested. I was asked if I understood. I was asked for my name and address, which I gave. (If you don't give this information, you can't be released on bail: you'll be kept in police cells until you go to court.) I was also asked for my date of birth and some other personal details, which I politely refused to give, though I couldn't resist giving my occupation as 'peace activist'.

There's no legal requirement to give any personal information to the police, and I didn't want to co-operate with the database state any more than I had to. This kind of information can be abused, in the way that our leaders abused their powers to create authoritarian laws and enter an illegal war. The sergeant tried to convince me that giving my date of birth was in my own interest, as it would speed up procedures. (Refusing didn't seem to delay us, as it turned out.) He claimed they'd find out eventually anyway. I still refused. Apart from the principle of the thing, deciding for yourself how much you are going to co-operate can help you feel stronger in a powerless situation.

Then the desk sergeant asked me: 'Are you willing to have your fingerprints taken?'

Unsure, I asked him: 'Are you *asking* me to have them taken, or are you *telling* me that I have to?'

He asked me again: 'Are you willing to have your fingerprints taken?' He made it sound as if it *was* necessary, so I agreed, and was taken downstairs to the fingerprint room. On the way there, I met Mil, who told me it was *not* a legal requirement for the offence I'd been arrested for. So I refused, and was taken back to the custody area.

After a while Mil joined me on the bench. He told me funny stories about being arrested to keep my spirits up. Once the paperwork had been done, he was led off to the men's cells. I was told I was going to 'Suite 14'.

I asked if I could keep my book. The sergeant looked at it (David Attenborough's *Life on Earth*), and said: 'Alright.' Then he asked me: 'What do you think about Iraq? Do you really think the troops should be withdrawn?'

I said: 'It's a complicated situation but I think we have to withdraw the US and British troops. They are not going to be able to create a peaceful democratic country there. I think it's unrealistic to hope that soldiers who have been in a war situation with a people can then switch roles to become a peacekeeping force. It's also asking a lot to expect an Iraqi to forgive and forget when they're confronted every day by a military force which has been responsible for the death of someone they loved, most likely a civilian. The continued involvement of US and British soldiers in Iraq is only going to add to the bloodshed.'

'At the same time,' I went on, 'it would be irresponsible for the West to just pull out of a country which we've plunged into civil war. One possible solution could be to replace US and UK troops with a more independent peacekeeping force, possibly the UN or the Arab League.'

I had the impression that the custody sergeant was genuinely interested in what I had to say, and genuinely confused about the best way forward for Iraq.

Then I was led downstairs to the women's wing. We passed closed cell doors with high-heeled shoes lined up outside. Outside 'Suite 14', I also had to take off my shoes—in case I decided to hang myself with my shoelaces. (Mil didn't have to do this.)

The door closed behind me. I was alone. Looking around the cell, I had a moment of panic. How would I cope with being confined in a stale, windowless room? (There was a 'window' made out of dense frosted glass bricks which let in some natural light, but no fresh air.) I was also worried about the fluorescent lighting, because after a while that kind of light makes me queasy. I looked around for a CCTV camera in the cell but I couldn't see one.

Then I calmed down. I wasn't being oppressed. The bed was covered in plastic, so it was probably quite clean. And I was on my own, not having to cope with other prisoners. I decided I had to be in strong survival mode. I lay down on the bed and started reading. The photographs of natural beauty were a real joy, taking me out of my surroundings.

After a while the hatch in the cell door flapped down, and a young Asian woman, the police nurse, asked me: 'Are you on medication or drugs? Or depressed?' No, no, no. As quickly as she'd appeared, she disappeared.

I fell asleep.

I think it is probably always like that after you get arrested. You have a very intense moment, with lots of adrenalin, and then afterwards you feel washed out.

I was woken up to be asked if I had any dietary requirements. I said I was vegan. By now I was completely disorientated about the time. There weren't any proper shadows, and you couldn't see through the window. There was a constant hum from some sort of generator (which was actually quite comforting). The main problem was the warehouse-like intense lighting.

After a while I received my lunch: some over-cooked yellow rice with rather sad vegetables and soggy chips. Gillian McKeith would've had a field day.

After another unknowable period of time, I was let out of the cell. It was 3pm, and I'd spent just over 5 hours in police custody (Mil had predicted 6). I was taken to the custody desk and charged with participating in an unauthorized demonstration. I said:

'Today I took part in a ceremony to remember an estimated 100,000 Iraqis and 97 British soldiers killed in the war with Iraq. The war was illegal and illegitimate. US and UK troops should be withdrawn immediately.'

Mil was waiting outside. Surprisingly, he hadn't been charged with 'organizing' our ceremony. They were waiting for instructions from the Crown Prosecution Service.

At that point I was the 20th person to have been charged with 'participating' in an unauthorized demonstration. I had no idea that I would be the first to be put on trial for this 'serious crime'.

Chapter 4

Peace Strike

1998-2003

As I came to the end of secondary school, I decided to continue following the path of education, applying to universities outside London. After being accepted by a few, I chose Liverpool University, because I wanted to live in a Northern city. I'd chosen history as my subject. I'm interested in the 'story' side of history, looking at a sequence of events and how they affect each other. Unfortunately, as I progressed with my degree, I realized that, although I loved the subject, I wasn't academically talented enough to pursue it as a career.

I enjoyed university life. I sang in the choir, and joined a women's football team. I liked the exercise involved in football, but I wasn't aggressive enough to keep possession of the ball. My attitude was more likely to be: 'You seem to want the ball more, so you should have it.' Throughout my three years at university, I lived in an all-woman household. For the first two years I was studious and lived a quiet life, not drinking alcohol, for example. It was only in my last year at college that I began going out with my friends to clubs and parties, and mixing with more creative and unreserved people.

One of the things I shared with my friends was music, which had always been part of my life. I have wide-ranging tastes. Music is one of the big pleasures in my life—even more than cooking, which I love. If you had to break down the happiness in my life, music might be 70 per cent of the total—listening to music, playing music, or thinking about music. The most important part of my music collection is my Bob Dylan collection. I have about eleven of his records, and six of his CDs.

I'd become aware of Dylan when I was sixteen, when I was going to Muslim classes. My teacher Ahmed had been a huge Dylan fan during his younger years, but he'd thrown out his records as a distraction from worshipping God. This didn't stop him talking excitedly about Dylan after class. Later, at university, I borrowed 'Blood on the Tracks' from a friend, and listened to the whole album five times in one night. From that moment on, Bob Dylan was a huge influence on me.

When I had to decide whether or not to take part in the Naming the Dead ceremony, Mil explained that if I was convicted and fined, and if I refused to pay the fine, I might have bailiffs trying to seize my property. Almost the only thing of value that I own is my music collection, which is probably worth over £1,000, though it's important to me because of the joy it gives me, not its monetary cost. It was a big decision to start down a path of action that might put at risk something so valuable to me.

After leaving university in the summer of 2001, I decided to stay on in Liverpool, living with the same group of friends, working in bars and living a pretty normal life based on going out to clubs and parties and socializing with my friends. I wasn't politically active in any way. My only political commitment was my veganism. So I was an ethical consumer in that sense, but I was not politically involved.

Even the shock of the 9/11 attacks did not make me want to be politically active. Watching the destruction of the Twin Towers that afternoon was appalling, and I felt enormous sadness that human beings had got to such a desperate point.

At the same time, I found it hard to feel hatred towards the terrorist group that carried out the attacks. I don't condone terrorist attacks at all, but I do think it is important to try to understand what could lead someone to carry out such a terrible action. Very large numbers of Muslims have died as a direct result of Western foreign policy over the decades, for example in Palestine and Iraq. In Iraq, hundreds of thousands of Muslim civilians died because of the economic sanctions imposed on the country from 1990 onwards. These kinds of policies have caused enormous anger in the Muslim world. I feel people turn to terrorism because of disempowerment, the sense that there is no other way to be heard.

I found the reaction from George W. Bush and Tony Blair in the days after 9/11 deeply depressing. I'm accused of being idealistic, but I continue to believe that there's no such thing as 'evil people'. There are people with mental health issues who fail to grasp the significance of their actions, and there are angry and hate-ridden people who inflict violence out of a desire for revenge. If someone hurts you, the natural response is to hurt them back. On 9/11, Al Qaeda were hitting back for the pain caused by the US to Muslim countries. That doesn't justify what they did in any way. It takes a strong, wise and righteous person to break the cycle of violence. 9/11 was the perfect opportunity for Bush and Blair to turn round and say: 'There are obviously some major problems in the world, let's stop the cycle of violence and sort things out. Let's find out why these people are so upset.' Sadly, this kind of Gandhi-type response is beyond our leaders, who are hypnotized by power, wealth and fame.

It wasn't until the invasion of Afghanistan that I started to feel the need to become active. I wasn't entirely certain about the real motivation behind the invasion, but I could sense that it was wrong and that it would only lead to a further escalation of violence. It was at this point that I joined my local anti-war group, Merseyside Stop the War.

I began attending meetings and helping to organize events. I met a lot of interesting and committed people, including Greg Dropkins, who was a draft resister from Chicago twice my age. Greg was an anarchist, but he never imposed his ideology on his peace movement work. I felt an affinity with Greg because of his careful, analytical and logical approach. We had many fascinating conversations, painting an enormous banner for the group or flyposting around Liverpool. Other people involved in the group were Tommy, an ex-docker; Joanne, my housemate; Jerry from CND; Muhammad from Palestine Solidarity Campaign; and the two Marks: Mark Holt, another former docker, and local solicitor Mark Henzel.

It was at these meetings that I was first confronted by my fear of public speaking. I had made presentations to seminar groups at university, but that was to small groups of people who I knew quite well. In the anti-war group, we were all expected to give our opinions on what the group was doing. When I was asked, I was petrified! I'd open my mouth and hope something intelligible would come out, but I had no control over what I was saying. I felt numb and detached, as though it wasn't me who was speaking. I just had no idea where the words were coming from. I just wanted it to end as soon as possible.

If it was ever suggested that I might do some public speaking, I would do pretty much anything to avoid it. I would be terrified that my mind would go blank and I'd be unable to speak, and that I'd be shaking visibly—especially if I was holding a bit of paper, which would be shaking. I have had the experience of being asked to say something in public, perhaps at a large organizing meeting, and being unable to string more than two sentences together. I'd say two or three sentences and end abruptly with: 'And that's all I have to say.' And people would look at me oddly for being so brief.

All the same, I was developing my own opinions, and my own understanding of what was going on in the world.

I was reading the newspapers on a daily basis for the first time in my life, and learning a lot through that. I would cut out particularly interesting articles and put them up on my wall. I was given a lot of Socialist Worker literature, because of my participation in the Stop The War group. The Socialist Workers' Party tried to recruit me a few times. I finally had to say to them: 'Look, I'm not going to join.' Their style of politics was too pushy for me, and I didn't really believe we were going to achieve a revolution. I felt change was going to come through a series of reforms.

So I was going to events and sometimes helping with the organizing, attending meetings, flyposting, and mixing with other like-minded individuals. In the spring of 2002, I helped organize a meeting at Liverpool University where Mil came to speak. I'd known Mil a long time, of course, through my cousin Emily. By this time he was a well-known anti-war activist. Other speakers included Lindsey German and John Rees from the Stop the War Coalition.

At this point I would say that a large proportion of people in the peace movement were not prepared for the invasion of Iraq. During his talk Mil described the situation in Iraq, and predicted that war would be declared on Iraq in a year's time, in the spring of 2003. Mil also explained the economic background to the impending war. He explained that the war was not about access to oil: whoever controlled oil would want to sell it. It wasn't about cheap oil, because if the price of oil was too low it would make the (expensive) oil that Britain and the US produced uncompetitive. It was about control of the profits that flow from the oil industry, and making sure that they went into propping up Western economies.

I was doing a lot of reading, but a lot of my understanding of what was going on came from the anti-war speakers who came to Liverpool. Apart from the University meeting, there was a big Stop The War rally in Liverpool with George Galloway and others delivering a passionate speeches. I have to say that Mil's talk at the University made more of an impression on me. It was focused on Iraq, and it was factual rather than based on emotion, and it made sense of the situation. It filled in a lot of the gaps for me.

Later, I went to the Voices in the Wilderness UK 'Resist!' conference in London, which helped to fill in more of the gaps. I also met some very inspiring people, such as Kelly Campbell and Ryan Amundson, who had come over from the USA. They had lost a family member in the Pentagon on 9/11, but they were now campaigning against war and retaliation in a relatives group called 'Peaceful Tomorrows'. After two days of talks and discussions at Kingsley Hall in the East End of London, I came away really feeling that I knew a lot more about the subject. I also got a book of Mil's called *War Plan Iraq*, that was published in September 2002, but I didn't read it before the invasion took place.

I didn't think Iraq had weapons of mass destruction or the potential to launch weapons in 45 minutes. Even if they had, I didn't think that was a justification for war. I thought the US and UK didn't give the UN weapons inspectors the opportunity to adequately inspect the country. The war came closer and closer, and there was a growing sense of despair in the anti-war movement. People all over the country began to prepare for what they would do in response to the invasion.

Merseyside Stop the War had decided on the contingency plan of demonstrating in Liverpool town centre if war against Iraq was declared. We planned to stop the traffic for a few hours on George Street in front of Lime Street Station.

It was mid-afternoon on 19 March when I learnt about the allies' decision to invade Iraq. There had been a national call for people to leave their work and protest when the war broke out. I was working that evening in a Mexican restaurant on Allerton Road opposite Penny Lane. My shift was due to start work at 5.30pm. Our demo was planned to start just before then, and continue for several hours. I phoned the manager and explained to him that as the invasion of Iraq had just taken place, I felt I had to be part of this protest. He told me that he expected to see me at the usual time. He didn't need to say that I was already on a final warning for lateness. I said again that Iraq had been invaded, I was going to take part in the protest.

I felt the invasion of Iraq was bigger than the opening time of a restaurant in Allerton. If someone had to wait longer for their *fajittah* because of the war then so be it. We should have all been in the streets protesting—managers, customers, cooks, everyone. Everyone in the city should have been out on the streets. Everyone in the country should have been out protesting, abandoning business as usual.

We were gathering at Lime Street Station. At 5pm, 30 of us marched into the middle of the road and stopped, holding our banners. One of the members of the STW group, Mark Holt stood in front of a slow-moving taxi. To my horror, the black cab started to slowly plough into Mark, who was now trying to physically push the cab back. I thought about sitting down in front of the cab, but when I saw it moving, I thought better of it.

After ten minutes, the police arrived, some of them on horseback. Now we were about 60 in number. I was starting to have second thoughts about what we were doing. We weren't winning anyone over. In fact it felt like we were making enemies of the people we were trying to gain sympathy from. Nevertheless, I'm glad I was part of it, because at that moment it was important to do something. A helicopter started circling above. After half an hour we moved off, marching through the town centre.

I finally left the demonstration for my job, which I was pretty sure I had lost. I felt I had a legitimate reason for being late, and I'd informed my employer with as much warning as possible. I was now two hours late. I pedalled furiously uphill to Allerton. Once inside, I approached the manager and looked him in the eye. He looked away and started fiddling with bits of paper. 'You no longer work here,' he said. I reminded him that my contract said: 'An employee is allowed to be late as long as he/she has a reasonable excuse e.g. a delayed train'. He was still looking away from me as he said: 'You don't have a reasonable excuse.' I was astounded by this. I said in a really shocked tone: 'What, protesting against the deaths of hundreds of thousands of people is not a reasonable excuse.' He looked up at me and said: 'No.' I stared him straight in the eye, and said 'Fine.' I walked out. This particular manager knew me well. He knew how important protesting against war was to me. Over the last year I had rearranged my hours many times to go on anti-war demos in London, and I'd been very vocal about the 'war on terror'.

Looking back on it, my small stand on 19 March was a kind of peace strike, a partial strike. I wish everyone had abandoned work on that day, and not only for two of their working hours. Perhaps then we could have brought this terrible war to an end sooner.

I cycled home from the restaurant. It was a real low point. War had been declared, protest didn't seemed to have worked, and I was now unemployed. I felt as if I'd lost my direction in life. As I cycled through Sefton Park, and the huge oak trees rustled, I thought about the bombs raining down on the Iraqi people at that exact moment. That put my problems into perspective. I had a safe home to return to, and my job didn't matter that much, especially if it stopped me from being able to protest on monumental occasions such as the outbreak of war.

Back home, I slumped down on the sofa, and watched the news. Baghdad was alight, burning with bombs.

Chapter 5

Bow Street

1 November 2005

From the outside, Bow Street Magistrates Court looked rather shabby. It was hard to believe that there was a court inside, it looked to me more like a block of flats. The first court on the site was in a private house, in the 1730s, but the current building was purpose-built in 1881. Six months after my trial, it shut down as a courtroom. I'd been told at the police station that my first hearing was at Bow Street a week later, on 1 November. I'd come into London the night before and stayed with Mum. She came to court with me in the morning, and we entered the building together, queueing up to pass through the metal detectors, and then looking around the lobby for my barrister.

When I'd been released from the police station, Mil had advised me to contact other people who were being prosecuted for 'participating in an unauthorized demonstration', and to be represented by the same lawyer as they were using. This turned out to be the solicitor Miranda Cohen at the human rights law firm Bindman & Partners. I went to see her the day before the hearing. As I walked into the lobby of Bindman's, I was impressed by the cuttings they displayed. I thought they must be a high-powered firm to have such high-profile cases. Miranda was really helpful, very clear and very professional. She told me what I already knew, that a lot of people had been arrested on the same charge before me, and that my trial would therefore probably come after the legal precedent had been set by one of these earlier cases. So I would just be processed by the system according to that precedent case. I was pleased to be just another one of the SOCPA cases. I was still doing something, helping to create pressure on the government, but I wasn't going to be THE case. I didn't want the pressure of being in the spotlight, or the responsibility of being the precedent case. Finally, Miranda told me my barrister was going to be Benjamin Narain.

After Mum and I found Benjamin in Bow Street, he went through what was going to happen, and we settled down to wait for my turn. My friend Jonathan Stevenson also turned up to support me, which I really appreciated, as it wasn't a very important hearing. All I was going to do was enter my plea of 'not guilty', and give my name and address. Then the court would set a date for the actual trial. Even so, I was still quite nervous—being the reason why all these people were in court, having to be ultra-respectful to the judge, and so on.

I was going to be in Court 1, on the ground floor, one of the largest courtrooms in the building. I went in and sat at the back, in the public gallery. There were cases of drunk and disorderly behaviour, begging, unpaid parking tickets. You heard little snippets of people's lives. A Scouser claimed he'd been begging to get a bit of food for the night, and he'd asked a police officer for 10p, 'and then I got nicked!' The way he told his story was really funny. The judge was sympathetic and said: 'Well, you've spent half a day in the cells, I think that's enough.' I started to relax a bit, because it was clear that judges are very intelligent, and this one seemed to be trying to be fair and compassionate.

Finally the usher called my name and I went into the courtroom proper and took the steps up into the dock. This is a sort of semi-caged bench, with wooden panels and black wrought iron enclosing it. It's quite a hard bench, and in that court there wasn't a lot of room for your knees.

Naming The Dead

The wood had graffitti written on it by past defendants. I did wonder, after having heard so many vivid stories in just a few hours, about all the other people who'd passed through that dock. I was facing the magistrate, who was behind a higher desk at the back of the court. I confirmed my name and address, and pleaded 'not guilty' to the charge of participating in an unauthorized demonstration. The legal argument we were planning to use was that section 132 of the Serious Organized Crime and Police Act (SOCPA) contravened the Human Rights Act, and therefore should not have been used to arrest me. This wasn't discussed at this hearing though, as we were just setting a date for the trial.

The judge asked the clerk for a date, and '7 December' was suggested. I knew that the first SOCPA trial wasn't due to take place until January, so I instantly knew that if this date went through, I'd be the first person on trial under this law. Benjamin said that he couldn't make that date, because he was away. Often, the date would have been delayed in order to accommodate him, which would have meant that I wouldn't be the first case. He asked for another date, but the judge was unsympathetic. The date stayed. So that was it. My first thought was: 'Holy cow! I'm going to be the first SOCPA case!'

I was told to leave the dock. Outside the courtroom, I turned to Benjamin: 'Oh my goodness, I've been put first.' He tried to reassure me: 'Don't worry, it's not going to be a big deal.' I was not comforted. Miranda, my solicitor, called me the next day to discuss it all. She said excitedly: 'You've been put first!' I responded worriedly: 'I know.'

I had serious doubts about being the first person on trial. I was worried that if my case was the precedent, I might jeopardize the trials of the other defendants. My case wasn't about defying the new legislation, it was about holding a remembrance ceremony which happened not to be authorized, whereas the four who were scheduled to be first on trial had been arrested at a specifically anti-

SOCPA demonstration. Mil and I discussed it, and we thought there might be a stronger argument for them to go first, as I was demonstrating for anti-war reasons and the arguments against SOCPA might not come across so powerfully in my trial. Perhaps I should try to delay my trial to let them still be the precedent case.

I consulted Emma Sangster, who has been a key person in the anti-SOCPA protests, and who was also a defendant. Emma didn't think that there was a problem, and she was very supportive of me being the precedent case. Emma actually played a big part in my decision to allow the case to go ahead on 7 December. If I hadn't spoken to her, I might have put pressure on Miranda to get the case put back. Emily Johns, my cousin, who's also involved in JNV, agreed it was a good idea for me to go ahead on 7 December, so I decided to just go with it.

I think the reason I was scheduled so quickly is that all the other cases involved several defendants. If four people are on trial, you have at least four police officers testifying, four defendants testifying, and maybe four defence lawyers making arguments. That could take a day and a half, or maybe two days. In my case, it was just one person on trial, which would take half a day, and there were just a lot more half-day slots available in the court schedule than there were one-and-a-half day slots. Now if Mil had been charged with an offence at the same time as I was, we might have been tried together, because the facts of our cases were the same, and my case would have been pushed back because it would have been a longer trial. But Mil wasn't charged with an offence until after my trial was over.

I *was* nervous about being the precedent case. But it was the same thing as when I knew I was going to be arrested. I said to myself: 'Right, be brave, you're doing this for an important reason, reasons which are more important than yourself. Having to stand in a courtroom is nothing compared to having your home bombed in Iraq. Just get a grip, you're going to do this.'

Chapter 6

Voices in the Wilderness

November 2003

For a month after the invasion of Iraq, I felt lost and alone. Merseyside Stop The War was fragmenting, and I stopped going to meetings. There didn't seem to be a contingency plan. The overwhelming feeling was: 'Well, we tried and it didn't work, so let's return to our everyday lives'. Then, six weeks after the invasion, a friend came by and asked if I wanted to join her on a trip to New York. I'd hardly ever left the UK, and I didn't have anything better to do. After she left, I cycled into town and got a new job working in a bar. Over the next three months, I worked solidly, into the early morning, saving for our trip to the USA. At this point, while I thought activism would be part of my life, I certainly didn't intend it to be the main focus of my life. When I left for the States in August 2003, it was in the spirit of adventure and fun.

But as soon as I arrived in New York it was impossible to escape politics or the media. The 'war on terror' was everywhere you looked. I was staying with friends in Maspeth, in Queens, a little way out from Manhattan. Our rooftop had a view of the Manhattan skyline. Our neighbourhood was full of posters supporting the troops in Iraq. Everyone knew someone who was stationed in Iraq. The US flag was absolutely everywhere—in every shop, in front of every house, on every street corner. Galleries exhibited art and photography inspired by 9/11. I saw a wall in Manhattan decorated with ceramic tiles which had been made by children—a 9/11 memorial. Most children had drawn flowers or sad faces, but one tile had a picture of a bearded man with the message: 'We're going to get you'. I was disturbed by this open commitment to revenge from a child, displayed for the whole world to see.

In my first week in New York, I had a small taste of what it might have been like to be in the city on 9/11. It was 14 August 2003, and I was on the subway. The train stopped at 12th Avenue. Then the engine of the train cut out and the lights went dead. There was a silence in my carriage. I remember thinking: 'Why have I come to the terrorist hotspot of the world? Why have I come here?' For a moment, everyone just sat completely still. There were no announcements or instructions. Then, after a while, all of the passengers got up. I had the feeling no one really wanted to venture off separately. I was thinking: 'Any minute now there'll be explosions. Why have I come here —of my own free will?' Eventually, we managed to make it up out of the station. It was a huge relief to be in the open air, but we were still all deeply confused. No one knew what was going on.

Amazingly, people on the street went into super-practical mode. At each intersection, people started standing in the middle of the road, directing traffic. The hustle and bustle of Manhattan suddenly transformed into a laid-back, slow-moving communal society. The only things which continued to work were the buses and cars. Still not really knowing exactly what was going on I continued my journey on foot. After two hours of walking, I stopped at a corner shop and bought a fruit salad. By now there was a carnival vibe on the street, people were hanging out and chatting. While munching on my papaya, mango and pineapple fruit salad I noticed a big clock on the side of a building still showing the time as 4.10pm, the same time the train had stopped on the subway. It was then I finally realized there must have been a power cut. The next day I read that 50 million Americans were without electricity that day, and there were 800 elevator rescues. Together with a friend I made outside the grocery store, I walked across Manhattan for the next six hours, talking about the 9/11 attacks, finally making it over the Brooklyn Bridge with a huge mass of people in the dark. A helicopter circled over our heads and shone a light down onto the crowd.

The solidarity shown during the power cut was part of the strong 'us against them' feeling in New York. A lot of people could tell something was not entirely right about the war on terror but most people I spoke to felt that the government was doing what it had to do to protect the country. I did come across other shades of opinion though. One afternoon as I was walking through Manhattan, on the West Side, I stumbled on an anti-war demonstration of about 500 people, totally surrounded by police. I joined in and walked with them for about an hour.

After six weeks of living in New York I decided to volunteer some of my time to a peace group. I had over a month left on my visa, so I contacted Mil, and he suggested Voices in the Wilderness in Chicago. Mil had known Voices for a long time, and had founded the British branch of the organization in 1998. I'd been to some Voices UK events, such as the Resist! conference in London.

Mil made the introductions, and two weeks later I was on a Greyhound bus taking the 19-hour ride to Chicago. I was greeted in Chicago by Scott Blackburn, a key member of Voices who became a good friend during my stay. Later that day I met Danny Muller, also a central figure in the Voices team. We also shared a strong affinity and had many long conversations about the peace movement. I also enjoyed spending time with Laurie Hasbrook, John Farrell and Angela Garcia who all worked in the office and who ensured that the group operated smoothly. While I was there I did some office admin for them, and went to a few conferences and talks. The other workers at Voices were a rich source of inspiration to me. They were people who I felt I had a genuine and strong affinity with, people I felt at home with.

I also met the co-founder of Voices, Kathy Kelly. Kathy is an intelligent, witty and compassionate woman who was (and still is) making tidal waves in the peace movement. I only met her a few times as she spends much of her time travelling around the country giving talks. I felt shy of her as she seemed superhuman. Underneath a black and white photograph of her in the Voices office, there was a caption saying she had been nominated for the Nobel Peace Prize four times. I was in awe of her. I didn't think anything someone like me had to say could be of any importance to someone like her. Kathy would be shocked to hear that, I know, because when we did speak, she was so light-hearted and humble: she would talk to anyone and value whatever they had to say.

I stayed with the Voices US team for one month. They were some of the most remarkable, intelligent, and compassionate people I've ever met. Their clear vision and practical approach to peace was both enlightening and reassuring. I had only ever worked with my regional anti-war group in Liverpool. Here were a group of people who had broken sanctions by taking medical supplies out to Iraq in person, who had stayed in Iraq during 'shock and awe', who were acting as a beacon to many the peace movement in the US and around the world. They were dynamic and intelligent, they were dedicating their lives to the movement and they were making a real difference.

After a month of volunteering with Voices, I'd come to the end of my visa, and I had to return to the UK. I had a new sense of purpose and direction to my life. Things were going to be different now.

Chapter 7

Serious Crimes

Brian Haw, Belmarsh and Beyond

The reason this book is being written is because of section 132 of the Serious Organized Crime and Police Act (2005), and there is one simple reason that law was passed. His name is Brian Haw. Brian is now internationally-known for his stand against Western brutality in Iraq. He has become a household name in Britain for his stand for free speech in Parliament Square, right in front of the Houses of Parliament. Brian, who is now 57, started his round-the-clock one-man protest in Parliament Square on 2 June 2001, first against the devastating economic sanctions on Iraq, and later against the 'war on terror' and the wars against Afghanistan and Iraq. In October 2002, Brian persuaded the High Court that he was simply exercising his right to freedom of speech, that his array of anti-war placards were not 'advertising', and that whatever obstruction of the pavement Brian and his display created was not 'unreasonable'.

When the Blair Government first introduced the Serious Organised Crime and Police Act (SOCPA), it allowed a senior police officer to remove someone from the vicinity of Parliament if that person was 'spoiling the visual aspect, or otherwise spoiling the enjoyment by a member of the public' of the area. If you failed to obey such an instruction to leave, you could be jailed for up to a year. This was a proposal directly aimed at Brian and his non-stop protest.

This was knocked out of the proposed legislation, but the government put in something even worse. They created a new offence of participating in, or organizing, an 'unauthorized demonstration' near the Houses of Parliament.

If you want to hold a public protest 'near' Parliament (and the area stretches out across the river even to the London Eye), then you must apply for permission at least 6 days in advance (or 24 hours, if 6 days is 'not reasonably practical'). The police are bound by the legislation to give permission for your event, but they have the power to impose conditions on:

(a) the place where the demonstration may, or may not, be carried on,
(b) the times at which it may be carried on,
(c) the period during which it may be carried on,
(d) the number of persons who may take part in it,
(e) the number and size of banners or placards used,
(f) maximum permissible noise levels.

So you might apply to hold an evening rally of 500 people in Parliament Square, but you might be told that you're only allowed to hold a breakfast-time vigil of 5 people under the London Eye. Displaying a single one-foot-square placard. For twenty minutes.

As Liberty, the human rights group, points out, these powers allow any demonstration 'to effectively be neutered'. If the organisers are told that only 500 people will be permitted, and they expect 1,000 to come, they might well cancel their protest in order not to risk breaching their conditions. The penalty for organizing an unauthorized demonstration is up to 51 weeks in prison, and a substantial fine. This is what Mil risked with our event.

The penalty for participating in an unauthorized demonstration is set in SOCPA as up to £1,000 in fines, plus court costs. When the SOCPA rules about demonstrations in the vicinity of Parliament came into force on 1 August 2005, there was a wave of resistance by groups and individuals who were determined to resist the new law. Four people were arrested at an unauthorized demonstration on 1 August itself, and others (including my friend Emma Sangster) were later arrested on anti-SOCPA 'people's picnics' in Parliament Square, and at other events.

During this whole time, Tony Blair and his ministers have boasted about the 'freedom' they've brought to Iraq, and the 'freedom' they defend in Britain itself. In April 2002, Tony Blair said: 'When I pass protestors every day at Downing Street, and believe me, you name it, they protest against it, I may not like what they call me, but I thank God they can. That's called freedom.' Brian Haw retorted: 'The Government doesn't want people to hear what I'm saying and to see the pictures of tortured and bombed innocent children which I have on display here.'

At first the law failed to affect Brian, because his protest was already in existence when SOCPA came into effect. Unfortunately, since May 2006 Brian has had to apply for authorization. However, at the time of writing he continues his resistance, and continues to be an inspiration to campaigners around the world. (You can read about his campaign at <www.parliament-square.org.uk>.)

One worrying tendency in recent years has been the use of anti-terrorism legislation to repress peaceful protests. During the first phase of the Iraq War in the spring of 2003, the government used the Terrorism Act 2000 against nonviolent demonstrators, including at the US military airbase at Fairford in Gloucestershire, which was being used to bomb Iraq. Soon after US B-52 bombers began arriving at the base at the beginning of March 2003, the Chief Constable of Gloucestershire used section 44 of the Terrorism Act 2000 to authorize police officers to stop and search people and vehicles across the whole of Gloucestershire *and* Wiltshire. In one amazing case, still being contested in court, the police commandeered coaches driving demonstrators from London to Fairford, and forced them to return to the capital without ever reaching the airbase. Terrorism legislation wasn't used in their case, but it was a frightening example of the right to demonstrate being removed in wartime.

Protesters at Fairford were stopped and searched half a dozen times every single day. That's not counter-terrorism, or even policing. That's just plain harassment. The Home Office admitted that between 21 February and 11 April 2003, the police conducted 995 stop and searches at Fairford—many of them under section 44 of the Terrorism Act. Police officers recorded that searches were carried out because they were 'looking for prohibited articles (tents) under s.44 of terrorism act', or because someone was 'wearing material which may cause damage to military establishment' or they were 'seen putting something in bag'. Terrorist tents, terrorist clothes, terrorist bags.

One of those stopped and searched under this 'anti-terrorism' legislation was 11-year-old Isabelle Ellis-Cockcroft. Terrorist children.

The most famous piece of 'terrorist' clothing so far was John Catt's T-shirt, worn to a protest at the 2005 Labour Party Conference. John, a war veteran then aged 80, wore a T-shirt saying: 'Bush Blair Sharon to be tried for war crimes torture human rights abuse'. Below this, it said: 'The leaders of rogue states'. Unbelievably, he was stopped by the Sussex police under section 44 of the Terrorism Act 2000. The stop-and-search form filled out by the police officer explained the reason for the search: 'carrying plackard [sic] and T-shirt with anti-Blair info' The purpose of the stop and search was said to be 'terrorism'. So, for the police, an anti-Blair slogan is a ground for suspecting terrorism, as law professor Marcel Berlins pointed out in the *Guardian*.

There have been plenty of other examples of terrorist clothing. At that same Labour Party Conference, it's said that a man was forced to change his T-shirt at a demonstration because it said: 'B-liar'. Over 600 people were stopped in and around that Labour Party Conference under section 44 of the Terrorism Act. None of them was charged with terrorism or any other crime.

The most famous person to be stopped under section 44 at the conference was of course the peace activist Walter Wolfgang. When the then Foreign Secretary Jack Straw claimed: 'We are in Iraq for one reason only: to help the elected Iraqi government build a secure, democratic and stable nation', Walter shouted out: 'Nonsense!' For this, the 82-year-old Walter was very roughly thrown out of the conference hall, despite being a delegate. When he tried to re-enter the building, the police detained him under section 44 of the Terrorism Act. This is only supposed to be used for stop someone and search them for terrorist items, but the police don't seem to have even bothered to search him.

I was lucky enough to meet Walter when he was putting together a Channel 4 documentary about the right to protest, and a group of protesters were invited to Brighton to be interviewed by him. Some of the other protesters were from 'Smash EDO' in Brighton, which campaigns against the arms company EDO (they make components for bombs and weapon systems used by the US and Israel). Smash EDO's right to protest was being suppressed not by anti-terrorist but by anti-stalking legislation (the 1997 Protection from Harassment Act). Fortunately, this was struck down by the High Court in May 2006.

Walter, John, Brian and I have all been fortunate enough to (so far) be left at liberty to continue our campaigns for peace and justice. However, in the most serious recent cases of human rights abuse in Britain, there are people who have been deprived of their liberty for years at a time, such as the sixteen refugees who were detained without charge in Belmarsh high-security prison. After 9/11, the government gave itself the power to detain foreign nationals indefinitely—without charge or trial—if they were suspected of involvement in terrorism. Imagine being locked up in a high-security prison without being told why you're being imprisoned, and unable to challenge the secret 'evidence' the government says it has against you. Belmarsh was rightly called 'Britain's Guantanamo'.

In one case, an Algerian man was put on trial for sending 'terrorist' items to Algeria. He was acquitted after arguing that he had been trying to help villagers who were being massacred in Algeria, by sending them things for their own self-defence. Despite the fact that he'd been acquitted, the government locked him up again after 9/11 using the same evidence that a jury had already rejected. The government admitted that he hadn't been observed to be doing anything terrorism-related since his release. They said this just meant that his methods of avoiding detection must have become more sophisticated!

If we don't have a scrap of evidence that you're guilty, you're still guilty, you're just really good at getting away with it. Everyone in the country could be locked up if this was the rule of law.

In December 2004, the Law Lords ruled that the Belmarsh system of detention without trial was not acceptable. Lord Hoffmann said: 'Terrorist violence, serious as it is, does not threaten our institutions of government or our existence as a civil community. The real threat to the life of the nation, in the sense of a people living in accordance with its traditional laws and political values, comes not from terrorism but from laws such as these.'

The sixteen detainess were released. But then they were put under a kind of 'house arrest' in a new punishment regime of 'control orders'. These 'control orders' limit your access to telephones and the internet, where you can go, when you're allowed to leave home, and who you're allowed to communicate with.

Imagine living under a curfew, with controls on who you can phone, who you can talk to, denied email or the internet, and all these controls are imposed without you being convicted of any crime, without you even knowing what your 'crime' is supposed to be.

Just before the invasion of Iraq in 2003, the government uncovered what it said was an 'Al Qaeda cell' involved in a 'ricin plot' in North London. There was then a massive police operation. More than 100 people were arrested and 26 countries were visited during a two-year investigation. When the case came to court, the seven-month trial revealed that no ricin had actually ever been found, and the jury decided that there had been no 'cell'. Only one out of the nine men was found guilty of anything. The other eight were released.

Despite the fact that they were found 'not guilty' or released for lack of evidence, these men continued to be targeted by the authorities, and several were re-arrested. Two were detained in Belmarsh again. Then, after Belmarsh was phased out, they were placed under 'control orders'.

Some of the jurors who had acquitted these men were so angry at the behaviour of the government that they spoke out against the re-detentions, and against the introduction of the new 'terrorism' legislation.

One juror told BBC's Panorama programme: 'Before the trial I had a lot of faith in the authorities to be making the right decisions on my behalf... having been through this trial I'm very sceptical now as to the real reasons why this new legislation is being pushed through.'

One juror said to the *Observer* newspaper: 'I was dumbfounded... During the trial there were clearly different degrees of evidence against different defendants. But in a couple of cases, the evidence was so flimsy you couldn't see where the arrest came from in the first place. To re-arrest them seemed totally unreasonable.'

The men are under control orders, but the High Court has said that control orders are a violation of the European Convention on Human Rights, so the government is in trouble there. Control orders can be imposed on anyone who is suspected of being involved, or having been involved, in 'terrorism-related activity'. So what is 'terrorism-related activity'?

The Terrorism Act 2000 broadened the meaning of 'terrorism'. Now, for example, it includes politically-motivated property damage. Take, for example, the Seeds of Hope Ploughshares action in 1996. Women went into a British Aerospace (now 'BAE Systems') factory, and hammered on a Hawk aircraft due to be exported to Indonesia, because they didn't want it to be used against the people of East Timor. They did 'serious damage to property', and they tried to 'influence the government' in Britain and in Indonesia, qualifying under the new definition of 'terrorism'. The women involved—Jo Blackman, Lotte Kronlid, Andrea Needham and Angie Zelter—admitted what they'd done, but were found 'not guilty' of criminal damage by a court in Liverpool, because of their argument that they were justified in stopping a crime being committed by the Indonesian government.

'Not guilty' of criminal damage. Guilty of 'terrorism'.

The Terrorism Act 2000 also made it a crime to have in your possession any information that is 'likely to be useful' to someone preparing an act of terrorism. It's not up to the prosecution to prove that you intended those photographs to be used for 'terrorism'. You have to prove that you are innocent. In August 2006, Rauf Abdullah Mohammed, an Iraqi Kurdish refugee living in London, managed to do this. He'd been prosecuted for making a video of London sights—allegedly for terrorist purposes. He was found 'not guilty' by a jury, but then immediately placed under control orders.

Everyone knows that since 9/11 the 'anti-terrorism' laws have mostly been used against Muslims. It's widely reported that 895 people were arrested under the Terrorism Act in the period up to October 2005, leading to only 23 convictions. Most of these arrests are believed to have been of Muslims.

According to the Metropolitan Police, in the two months after the 7 July attacks, of the people stopped in the streets of London under section 44 of the Terrorism Act 2000,

27 per cent were Asians, even though Asians make up only 12 per cent of London's population. Anti-terror stops on vehicles rose by 86 per cent for white drivers, by 108 per cent for Afro-Caribbean drivers and by 193 per cent for Asian drivers. The use of anti-terror stop and search powers against Afro-Caribbean and Asian pedestrians increased 1,100 per cent compared to a year earlier.

A member of the Metropolitan Police Authority, Peter Herbert, said: 'Intelligence cannot lead to a 1,100% increase, this is just random stop and search.' Making random stops 'deter no one', 'alienate large numbers of people' and 'waste time and resources,' he added.

In June 2004, a year before the crisis caused by the 7/7 bombings, the human rights group Liberty wrote:

> Police powers have been used disproportionately against the Muslim population in the UK. The majority of arrests have been of Muslims, a large number of whom were subsequently released without charge, or charged with offences unrelated to terrorism. All of those detained indefinitely have been Muslim men. The way in which anti-terror laws are being used has led to feelings of isolation amongst many of the 1.6 million Muslims in the UK.

Liberty said that the government was effectively 'criminalizing' Muslims as a community: 'The group as a whole is stigmatized, and Muslims have often described themselves as feeling "under siege".'

We don't have space to go into the British government's involvement in the CIA 'extraordinary rendition' secret-prison-torture-transportation system, or its collaboration with the Guantanamo regime (documented by former prisoner, Moazzam Begg, in his wonderful book *Enemy Combatant*). All these repressive policies help to make Muslims feel their community is under attack.

As well as the established human rights groups like Liberty, there is a grassroots campaign against new repressive laws called the 'Campaign Against Criminalizing Communities', which brings together non-Muslims and Muslims in challenging the erosion of freedom in Britain. It brings together the cases of the Fairford protesters, Mohammed Abdul Kahar, the Muslim man shot in the fruitless Forest Gate raid, the Parliament Square picnickers, and so on.

I should point out that SOCPA did a lot more than just restrict protests around Parliament. Among other things, it brought in two new laws aimed specifically at animal rights campaigners, and made a crime out of 'harassment', which is defined as trying to persuade someone to do something they don't have to do, or not to do something they are legally entitled to do. As George Monbiot points out, 'there is no defence for peaceful protest'.

SOCPA also created the new offence of trespassing on 'national security' sites. (It didn't define what 'national security' means.) The first sites named were mostly to do with nuclear weapons, including Menwith Hill, the US/UK spy base in North Yorkshire.

When this part of SOCPA came into effect in April 2006, Helen John, 68, and Sylvia Boyes, 62, both Greenham Common women in the 1980s, broke into Menwith Hill base, 'armed' with a small pair of boltcutters and a hammer, to deliberately challenge this new law. They knowingly risked up to a year in prison and a £5,000 fine.

Sylvia, who was found 'not guilty' of causing criminal damage to a British nuclear submarine in 1999, said:

> I am quite willing to break the law and prepared to be charged and to go to prison. The Government thinks it can do whatever it wants and that it has a passive public which accepts whatever it throws at it. I find it very worrying.

Sylvia and Helen were arrested, but they have not been prosecuted—yet—despite another 'entry' in June 2006.

We need people like Sylvia and Helen—and all the other fine people who campaign against injustice and war. By working together, we can resist and overturn the government's serious crimes against peace and freedom.

Chapter 8

Justice Not Vengeance

November 2003–July 2005

After my exhilarating time in Chicago with Voices in the Wilderness, I arrived back in Britain absolutely inspired. I wanted to carry on campaigning. It felt almost like a calling. I called Mil and said I would like to move down to Hastings to do an internship with his peace organization Justice Not Vengeance for six months. He suggested we met face-to-face to talk about it.

I met Mil at a greasy spoon café near London Bridge, and he tried his best to put me off! He wanted me to be sure that it really was the best thing for me to do. He asked me to be clear about what I wanted to achieve. This is what I wrote:

Work Objectives of Maya Evans with JNV

Goals
1. Make a positive difference to the world.
2. Expand skills base. This includes technical know-how with computers, cameras and recording equipment. Improve literary skills, the ability to research accurately and relevantly. The ability to write up findings or ideas to a high standard. To become competent in the ability to write, this may be in pressured situations and/or creatively.
3. Build on political and general knowledge of domestic and international affairs.

4. Become better at verbally expressing myself, especially in public situations in front of audiences and on the spot. I want to be able to speak both analytically and creatively in a confident manner.

Looking at it now, I feel I've come close to achieving quite a few of these goals. I'm surprised how much I have done.

Mil and Emily live in St Leonards-on-Sea, part of Hastings, and I found a flat a few minutes away from them. It was the first time I'd ever lived on my own. My first six months in Hastings was really tough, financially and emotionally. Financially, I was trying to find a job (JNV couldn't pay wages), and emotionally I was recovering from a broken relationship in Liverpool. Gradually, however, I became more involved in the Hastings scene and made new friends, and I became more involved in JNV and anti-war work. That included campaigning with the local group, Hastings Against War (HAW). (We once sent a message of solidarity to Brian which said 'HAW supports Haw'.) I've benefited a lot from the experience and friendship of the committed members of HAW, including Rona Drennan, my running partner John Enefer, Fernando Bauza, my namesake Maya Goia, Jim Wright, George Moles, Bill Penn of the Friends Meeting House, John Lynes who puts his life on the line in Palestine, Jenny Allan, and of course Emily.

One important turning point in my development as an activist came in August 2004, when HAW protested against the 'Airbourne' airshow in Eastbourne, a few miles along the coast from Hastings. We'd been invited to join in a campaign against Airbourne started by Eastbourne activist Ruth Winbourne. Up to that point, my main involvement with HAW had been doing the Saturday stall in town, writing letters, helping to organize speaker meetings and so on. Now we had been invited to help campaign against the weekend 'celebrations'. Military aircraft, flying killing machines, were being dressed up as a family day out, an entertainment. It was helping to make war socially acceptable. The fighter planes fly over the crowds in formation, while a Radio 1-style DJ announces on a loudspeaker the names of the planes and their capabilities. He doesn't announce how many bombs they can drop, or when they have been used in combat, or how many lives they have destroyed. The jets zoom overhead with a huge roaring sound following a few seconds later, and it feels like what it would be like for someone moments before a bomb is dropped on them. If you were being attacked, it would be a very frightening and bewildering noise, perhaps the last sound you'd hear as your home and everything you know in life was destroyed. I found it very moving to be at Airbourne and think on the victims of war.

I'd say the majority of those who attend the event haven't thought much about the true use of these planes. It was our intention to try to make people think about that reality. HAW decided to visit Airbourne for the day and to hand out flyers which were designed to look like official pamphlets for the event. They just gave a little bit more information than the usual leaflet, for example explaining that the Hawk jets on display were sold to Indonesia in the 1990s to commit genocide in East Timor.

The seven of us were also going to unfold a large banner reading: 'These planes drop bombs. Bombs kill people.' After leafleting the crowds, we made our way to the end of Eastbourne pier. We'd decided that just after 3pm, when the Tornados were due to fly in formation past the end of the pier, the crowds would be looking in our direction. At the agreed time, we released the banner over the balcony of the clock tower. The security guards marched up, snatched the banner away and proceeded to remove us from the pier.

The crowds around us were very hostile. Despite this, some members of the group continued the protest by shouting out our message: 'These planes drop bombs! Bombs kill people!' I was very reluctant to join in. I was thinking: 'I can't do something so confrontational when the majority of people are against us'. Then a Tornado flew overhead. The thundering noise made me think of other people who have heard that sound, who have had their homes and communities destroyed. I felt rage. I began storming down the pier, shouting out our message, with a conviction that surprised everyone including me. (I was told later that before the demonstration I'd seemed very apprehensive about taking part.)

My work in JNV revolved around compiling an events calendar and emailing it to our list of about 3000 people, updating our website, dealing with administration, outreach to anti-war groups and organizing some events.

The main project I was involved with up until the spring of 2005 was 'Counter Terror: Build Justice'. The idea behind this was summed up in our statement, which was signed by dozens of groups including the Green Party UK, Pax Christi UK, and Voices in the Wilderness in both the US and Britain. Prominent individuals also signed, including Noam Chomsky.

The 'Counter Terror: Build Justice' statement said:

> In the face of global terrorism, we believe that our community, our nation, and our world, must choose the path of peace, human rights, and justice.
>
> We believe that what is presented to us as 'the war on terrorism' is a campaign of violence and repression that actually generates more anti-Western terrorism…
>
> We believe that the scale of anti-Western terrorism will only be reduced by resolving the legitimate grievances which terrorism springs from. We believe that peace will only come through justice.

The statement also addressed the problems of weapons of mass destruction and corporate globalization. It ended:

> In the event of a major terrorist attack against our country, we commit ourselves to supporting victims and their relatives, defending the rights of those threatened by a vengeful backlash—particularly Muslims and Arab people in our com-

munities, and nonviolently resisting any military response by our government.

In early 2004, Voices US invited me to come over and work in their office again. I was able to promote 'Counter Terror, Build Justice' while I was there, for example at a national anti-war networking conference in Bloomington, Indiana. I learned about a lot of things, including about depleted uranium (DU). DU is twice as heavy as lead and is used in anti-tank shells by the US and UK. When fired into a vehicle, the DU ignites and forms an 'aerosol' of tiny radioactive particles which can be inhaled or eaten, and then cause long-term health problems. DU takes hundreds of years to break down. It is easily absorbed into the ecosystem by animals eating plants contaminated by the substance. I heard that over 320 tons of DU were fired in Iraq and Kuwait in the 1991 war, and over 1,750 tons of DU ordnance were fired in Iraq in the spring of 2003. I found this shocking information.

Throughout the conference I was speaking with small groups and individuals about 'Counter Terror: Build Justice'. Many people seemed enthusiastic about being involved and taking part. I was facing up to my anxiety about public speaking. As I said earlier, when it is my turn to say something, all the words fly out of my head, I start to feel dizzy and my face feels hot. Then I was invited onto the platform to say a few words about the campaign. I think they were expecting a rousing speech but I knew I wasn't capable of that. I had thought about what I was going to say and had run through it a few times in my head. Now I went up and stood on the platform in a lecture room in front of 100 people, trying to sell an idea. It was the first time I'd tried real public speaking. I started off well, introducing the campaign and when it was set to run. I was projecting my voice, but my words were not flowing smoothly. I was stuttering a lot. I felt uncomfortable with being the centre of attention. My knees were shaking. I looked up. An elderly gentleman in the front row was nodding off. I thought:

'Oh my God, I'm losing them. Just as I thought, no one is interested in what I have to say and the way I'm saying it'. I dried up. There was a deadly silence in the hall which seemed to go on and on. I quickly ran through the remaining points and ended by saying rapidly in a flat voice: 'It would be really nice if you would all consider joining us in this campaign'. I was so relieved to hurry back to my seat and sit down. What a nightmare, but at least it was over and I had kind of got through it. The woman next to me leaned over and whispered: 'I just love the English accent'. I couldn't believe she hadn't noticed I was boiling on the spot and was about to keel over.

It's strange but the English accent in the USA does give you credibility. I was asked on several occasions by the Voices team to read something or say a few words at events, because of my accent. It was a huge confidence boost for me. Also, possibly if you have come from another country on a mission, people take you more seriously and think you have conviction and you mean business. In any event, it was the first time in my life I was regularly the centre of attention, and I was getting used to it—in probably the most supportive environment possible.

After a month in the US, I returned to St Leonards, moved into Stanhope Place with my best friend Raquel, began volunteering at the Electric Palace cinema, and started working in Trinity Wholefoods. Apart from serving in the shop, I had the opportunity to prepare food for sale (sandwiches, nutroasts, stuffed peppers, cakes and salads), and the soups in particular became my responsibility. When customers started complimenting me, and making a point of asking if I'd cooked the soups, I was taken aback, and then really pleased.

I started becoming interested in cooking in my midteens when I started taking responsibility for my own meals. I also loved going round to my friends' houses and learning how to cook curry. My friends' mothers were some of the best cooks I've ever met, and were careful to cater for my

Naming The Dead

veganism with their dhals and sag aloos. It was during this time I realised how certain flavour groups combined well together and how you can bring out those flavours. I then started experimenting, putting unlikely ingredients together. Making nice food is one of the best things one person can do for another. A good meal always cheers people up.

Hastings was starting to feel like home. I love living by the sea, and more importantly, after Liverpool, I love living near part of my family. I still value more than anything having a family base. My family have given me everything I have achieved to date.

The Counter Terror: Build Justice project continued into March/April 2005. In some ways, it was a difficult time, because we were reaching out to anti-war groups, and many of the phone numbers we had were of people who weren't active in the movement any more. The anti-war movement felt in decline. A positive side of the project, however, was putting together our Counter Terror: Build Justice documentary, which we made in January 2005. Mil and I had been talking about it for a while, but we didn't feel we had all the skills needed to put something together quickly. Then we persuaded a local activist called Dave Palmer to be involved, and to contribute his camera and video editing skills. Dave is also a vegan as it happens, and actually worked in the Vegan Society, which was based in St Leonards at the time. I arranged interviews with our local MP, Michael Foster; with one of the leading Muslim figures in Hastings, Dr Tariq Rajbee; and with leading peace activist Bruce Kent. I interviewed people in the street, and I was also involved in the editing of the documentary, which was a very intense process. I feel proud to have been involved, and the documentary still seems relevant to what is happening today.

The one thing that I found shocking during the making of 'Counter Terror: Build Justice' was when our Blairite MP, Michael Foster, declared that people become terrorists because they are 'evil'. To me that doesn't make sense. No one is born 'evil'. You meet mean people in life but those people have usually had a difficult background. I don't condone acts of terrorism by any means, but I can understand why a Palestinian might commit an act of terrorism after seeing an unarmed Muslim gunned down on the street by Israelis who have the financial and political support of the USA. If people feel helpless, they lash out. To me it makes sense to look at why people feel a certain way and try to resolve the issues they have.

Dr Rajbee told us the story of the Prophet Muhammad returning from a battle with his men, and telling them that they had to now fight the greater *jihad*, the battle within, overcoming selfishness. Most of the Muslims I've talked to are appalled by the inaccurate use of the word *jihad* by both the media and the terrorists. It just means 'struggle'.

During our month of action, March-April 2005, some groups who'd signed up to Counter Terror: Build Justice carried out activities varying from showing the documentary to holding a stall, to having a night of discussion. The month of action didn't achieve what we'd hoped it would, largely because the anti-war movement had fallen into something of a depression. Many people concluded that if a demonstration of one and a half million was not enough to stop a war, then any form of people power was a waste of time.

To be honest, I often have moments of doubt about the work that I commit a large amount of my time to. I felt that very strongly in the year after the invasion of Iraq. I think what kept me going was mixing with other dedicated activists, and continuing to be a dreamer, to live in hope. I also tried to keep a focus on the bigger picture.

Peace work isn't just about changing a country's foreign policy, it's also about reinforcing the idea that violence is not a method of resolving a problem. It's about creating a culture of peace.

Chapter 9

Strip Search

July–August 2005

I first heard about the Hiroshima Peacewalk in December 2004. A Belgian peace and environmental organization called 'For Mother Earth' emailed JNV, asking us to promote the walk, which was to mark the 60th anniversary of the bombing of Hiroshima on 6 August 1945. I put the dates on our website and wrote back with our best wishes. I'd always wanted to go on a peace walk, and this sounded the perfect opportunity. At the time, I had no idea what an important experience the walk was to be for me.

Over the next few months I saved money from my job at Trinity Wholefoods. I didn't know anyone else who wanted to take part, so I went by myself, crossing the Channel, then catching buses and trains to meet the others. The walk was supported by the organization 'Mayors for Peace', started by the Mayor of Hiroshima in 1982. Mayors across the world have pledged their towns as 'peace towns'. Thanks mainly to 'For Mother Earth', more than 200 towns in Belgium have signed up. Our two-week peace walk involved stopping off at many of these towns for official receptions. Our final destination was Kleine Brogel, where there is a North Atlantic Treaty Organization (NATO) base housing US nuclear weapons. NATO is committed to the first use of nuclear weapons, and links non-nuclear European countries like Belgium with the nuclear arsenals of the US, Britain and France. In Kleine Brogel there are 20 US B-61 nuclear bombs, which can be set to an explosive force of up to 170 kilotons. The Hiroshima bomb, which killed around 100,000 people, had an explosive force of 12.5 kilotons.

The number of walkers went up to 35 at one point, but the hard core was just 15 of us. It was a very bonding experience, walking in all weathers, sometimes for ten hours a day. It was also a wonderful experience for me, with intense conversations with great people from across the world, as well as solitary moments for reflection. While walking, we folded 1,000 'peace cranes'. There is an ancient Japanese tradition that if you fold 1,000 of these origami birds, you will have your wish granted. A Japanese girl called Sadako Sasaki, who was two years old when Hiroshima was bombed, developed leukemia as a result of the attack when she was 11 years old. Sadako tried to fold 1,000 cranes to try to make herself better, but still died of cancer on 31 October 1955. 'Peace cranes' have now become a symbol of resistance to nuclear destruction.

On average, we covered 25km a day, camping each night on land provided by the local council. We'd get up at 7am, eat breakfast, then walk to the next town. We might stop in three towns a day. The receptions were lavish, offering local beers, meats and cheeses. After the first few days, I stuck to orange juice. The mayor would welcome us, and then our representative, Mr Yoshio Sato, would speak.

Mr Sato, who was 74, was a *hibakusha*, a Hiroshima survivor. He would describe what happened in Hiroshima on the day that the US dropped the atomic bomb. (Mil tells me that Britain was also involved in the decision.) Mr Sato was 14 when they dropped the bomb, and he was one kilometre away from Ground Zero. Mr Sato was relatively unharmed, but he saw people being transported on wagons, and their skin was peeling off. Mr Sato had drawn pictures of what he'd seen, and he would show these pictures to the mayor, to the audience and to the press. His father was away on a business trip, so Mr Sato was at home with his brother, his mother and his sister. His sister, who was about 6, died a month after the bombing. His mother passed away a year later from radiation sickness. His brother died of cancer, but not till later in life. Mr Sato's own hair fell out a few months after the bombing. Then later in life he'd developed cancer himself, requiring the removal of half of his stomach.

Everybody on the peace walk was very supportive of Mr Sato, recognizing the strength that it took to give that talk two or three times a day. Mr Sato used his experiences in a positive way, without self-pity or anger. We all had the utmost respect for him. At the same time, it was extremely draining to hear his horrifying story several times a day. It made our reason for walking much more real.

Gradually I realized that there were going to be civil disobedience actions later in the walk. While civil disobedience was something I thought I might be involved in one day, it wasn't something I felt very strongly drawn to. I can remember one experience during a protest in London in April 2004 organized by Voices in the Wilderness UK and others. A conference was taking place for corporations seeking to profit from the occupation of Iraq, shortly after the first major assault on Fallujah. We were protesting outside a restaurant where they were holding a gala dinner, and feelings were running high. A rumour went around that an attempt was going to be made to enter the building and disrupt the dinner. I felt very strongly that this was not for me. Going to court and having a criminal record, being barred from certain jobs, and possibly suffering damage to my credit rating, all added up to a big commitment. I also shrank from the rough and tumble aspect.

Over a year later, on the walk, I'd become a little bit more open-minded about civil disobedience, but it was not a priority for me. When people started talking about doing civil disobedience on the walk, I was not instantly drawn to it. Especially when I heard how a year earlier people from the group had broken into an airbase in the middle of the night, and been chased through forests by armed guards. I thought: 'No way! That's not for me!'

But things changed. I developed a great deal of trust in my fellow walkers. I listened day after day to Mr Sato's testimony. I felt more and more strongly about what we were doing. I was living and breathing the campaign against nuclear weapons. It had become my whole world. I began to be more open to the idea of civil disobedience, partly because of my talks with David Heller of For Mother Earth, and Jane Tallents from Scotland. Both were experienced activists who had been arrested many times. Jane is involved with Faslane peace camp, which campaigns against the Trident nuclear submarine base just north of Glasgow. She is an energetic, cheerful, long-term activist who's been arrested over 50 times, and who's even been to prison for protesting against nuclear weapons. Her son Sam was also on the walk. He was only 19 at the time I met him, but he'd already been arrested several times for peaceful protests, which I found very challenging. If even a 19-year-old could make this kind of commitment... It felt like there was a line there between being a bystander and being someone who seriously believes in what they're doing.

The action was going to be at NATO's European headquarters in Brussels. First we would just leaflet staff going into the base and passers-by about nuclear weapons. The police had said that we could stand outside the main gate of the base to do this. Then we would carry out some nonviolent arrestable action.

We developed our ideas during a three-day camp on the outskirts of Brussels, in a vicar's garden. At an all-day nonviolent direct action (NVDA) workshop, we discussed what we could possibly do at the base, how we felt about 'breaking the law', and the possible repercussions. (From one point of view, it is the nuclear weapons that are illegal, and our peaceful actions to get rid of them are legally justified.) We were told that it was very unlikely that we

Naming The Dead

would end up with a 'proper' arrest and a criminal record. We would probably have an 'administrative arrest', which is just a temporary detention. As for the action, it was first suggested we might climb the fence around the base and risk the guard dogs. I was not keen on this idea at all, as I am really bad at climbing, I was afraid of the barbed wire involved, and I was pretty alarmed at the idea of having a dog wrestle me to the ground. The idea we settled on was to form a human blockade in front of the main entrance, to symbolically stop workers from entering and leaving NATO. I felt more inclined to take part in this action as it involved making a stand while not being too dangerous.

In the afternoon, we split up. One group was of people who were *likely* to participate in civil disobedience, and the other was made up of people who probably wouldn't. It was left very open for people to change their minds.

I decided to join the action group. I felt the action wouldn't harm anyone, wouldn't be dangerous for us taking part, and was the kind of thing that shouldn't be illegal. I wouldn't have considered taking part if there had been a high risk of ending up with a criminal record, especially because it would have meant travelling back to Belgium for any trial. We were going to work in 'affinity groups', small groups of people you trusted and would feel comfortable being arrested with. In a way, the walk had helped the whole group to develop into one large affinity group.

The next morning several of us dressed in white boiler suits, as 'citizen weapons inspectors'. We were joined by other activists, including a branch of the 'Clandestine Insurgent Rebel Clown Army', an activist group that uses clowning as part of its campaigning. Altogether there were about 60 of us as we walked to NATO headquarters. When we got there, we found that the police had gone back on their agreement and they were not allowing us to stand next to the base entrance. We were across the road from the base, on the other side of a dual-carriageway, with armed police guarding us.

Our small delegation went into the base, led by Mr Sato and accompanied by Bruno de Lille, the Green deputy mayor of Brussels. They talked to a high-level official in NATO while those of us outside broke into different affinity groups. I was in a group with Jane and Sam and some Swedish people. When our delegation came out of the camp, we pretended that we were leaving the area. The 'Clandestine Insurgent Rebel Clown Army' then led us across the highway. A row of armed men in black ran towards us, grabbing the clowns. I kept marching across the road. I had a string of peace cranes I was determined to hang on the fence. I kept walking, until I was further across the road than anyone else. Then someone pushed me to the ground from behind and twisted my hands up behind my back, tying them with cable ties. I was pulled to my feet, and I went limp. This is what we'd agreed at our NVDA workshop. More police carried me over to the police van and threw me in. The others were brought in, which was an enormous relief. The Clown Army were cracking jokes, using feather dusters to tickle the police through the iron bars, and making siren noises as we barrelled through the streets. By the time we arrived at the police station we were all giggling. My only worry was that my hands were tied so tightly they were going cold. By the time the ties were cut off, minutes after we got to the police station, I was quite upset, because I couldn't feel my hands any more.

Then one of the female police officers led me off to another room. We were alone. She ordered: 'Take off all your clothes.' I was thinking: 'Oh my God! This was not in the NVDA training session!' I asked her: 'Are you sure?' She was sure. I took my clothes off down to my underwear. She said: 'Take all your clothes off.' I was thinking: 'This is not happening.' I realized she wasn't joking. I turned round and took my underwear off. She told me to put my clothes back on, and another female police officer led me back to the others. They were all led off one-by-one to be strip-searched.

Because there were such strong women in the group, they helped me to deal with the experience. The two clown women told us they'd done a striptease, throwing their underwear around. Jane, who's been arrested many times, had never been strip searched, but wasn't troubled by it. The Swedish girl was also fine about taking her clothes off. We decided it had been done to undermine us, not because of any real security concerns. We found out later that one of the male clowns even managed to take cigarettes and a lighter into his prison cell.

Hours later, after we'd slept, we were released onto the streets of Brussels. I felt jubilant and empowered, but also dazed. When we got back to the church, we were met with cheers, and a lovely meal laid on by Rampenplan, a Dutch vegan catering collective. We were told that Bruno de Lille had been annoyed, because our action distracted attention from the delegation. It's true that the press (as far away as Austria) focused on the civil disobedience. But I don't think the delegation, which emerged without any promises from NATO, would have made the news.

The next day, I talked to Jane about it all: I really appreciated the chance to talk to an experienced and caring activist. Apart from it being my first arrest, I'm not used to being shoved around, and I'd been shocked by the strip search. I felt shaken up by the experience. I think affinity groups should always have evaluations after actions so that people can talk about their feelings. If I'd been by myself, without support, I'd have been really traumatized. As it was, I felt strange for two or three days afterwards. When I look back on it now, though, my overall feeling about the whole experience is positive.

A week later, the last stop on the walk was Kleine Brogel, where we held a remembrance ceremony for the people of Hiroshima in a local church. It was 6 August, the anniversary of the attack. Walkers spoke, Mr Sato spoke, and the mayor spoke, all calling for an end to nuclear weapons and war. We then walked to the base, and held a die-in. We lay down in the middle of the entrance at the exact time of day that the bomb destroyed Hiroshima. We lay there still and silent for five minutes. Afterwards, the guards seemed confused. I took part in the die-in to try to make the soldiers think about the other side of the argument, and to show solidarity with those who died in the bombing of Hiroshima, and in all wars. I thought about those who have lost loved ones through war. Nobody should have to endure that kind of sadness, especially now when wars are fought for profits and global domination.

The bombing of Hiroshima still affects people today, mentally and physically. Meeting Mr Sato brought home to me the reality of war. We don't tolerate murder, and we shouldn't tolerate the murder of people through war.

That was the end of the walk. After spending two weeks with people who had become my family, leaving was really difficult.

I think I developed a lot as a person as a result of the walk. Without the Hiroshima Peacewalk, I don't know if I would have had the strength to take part in the Naming the Dead ceremony. One of my best memories was when I was asked to co-facilitate the biggest meeting of the walk, with over 30 activists from around the world, all with different agendas. Afterwards people were really appreciative. One person asked if I could facilitate all of the meetings. After all my fears of public speaking, I really appreciated their confidence. A lot of what I know about facilitating I've learned through being involved in Hastings Against War, facilitating meetings, and going to Emily's facilitation workshop. The most important thing I've learnt is to allow everyone to feel that they have had their say and that they've been respected, but at the same time not let any one individual dominate or undermine others.

I'd changed as a person. I was ready for the next step, though I didn't know it at the time.

Naming The Dead

Chapter 10

Convicted

7 December 2005

On the day of the trial, I got up early while it was still dark. I had a bath and put on my black clothes because they were the most serious ones I had. When I left the house it was still pitch black. I walked to the station, and then just looked at my notes all the way to London on the train, practising what I was going to say at the trial. I really wanted my evidence on the stand to be as powerful as possible, because that is the one opportunity you get to make your point and everyone is listening to you. I really wanted to do a good job.

The week before the trial, I had a session with Emily which was really helpful. Emily took me through the concluding statement that the lawyers had drawn up for the trial, and we prepared something for me to say on each of their points, when I was giving evidence. I prepared for that, and I memorized some statistics. Looking over my papers reminded me of being at school, looking over my notes before an exam. I was 'cramming' on the train.

I got to London about 8.30am. I arrived at the court super-early at about 9am. There were photographers already there, but I didn't want to go over and introduce myself as the person whose case was on that day. I just stood around while Gabriel and Mil and other supporters turned up. Mil, who was my only defence witness, had come overnight on the Eurostar from an international meeting in Amsterdam.

The 'SOCPA gang' came—people who were going to be on trial themselves soon for the same 'crime', including Emma Sangster, Maria Gallestegui, David King, Mark Barrett, Prasanth Visweswaran, Chris Coverdale, and Aqil Shaer. Other friends of mine from the anti-war movement that I remember seeing were David Polden, Richard Crump —the anti-war poet, Jonathan Stevenson, who'd been at the first hearing as well, and Peggy Preston. Molly Cooper and Rikki, who'd taken photos and video of the remembrance ceremony, were also there.

A lot of the SOCPA defendants who were involved in the anti-SOCPA group 'People in Common' now set up banners and held a bell-ringing ceremony, reading out a list of Iraqi and British names. My uncle John came, and rang a bell. Mum showed up and took part as well. It was really nice to have this ceremony, a re-enactment of why I was on trial. I suppose for the journalists it reinforced how peaceful the action was. Mainly, it created the kind of solemn atmosphere that we'd had when we were reading names, the sense of sadness and loss.

Waiting outside the courthouse, I felt calm and nervous at the same time. After a while, journalists began approaching me for interviews. My new barrister Alisdair Mackenzie arrived and drew me away to talk about the case. Alisdair was very calm and a really nice person. We ran through some of the questions he was going to ask me. Then there was still time before the trial started, so I went outside to be interviewed by the journalists who were waiting to talk to me. It took so long that I was actually one of the last people from our group to go into Bow Street. As we were going up the stairs, Alisdair said: 'Oh, is that Brian Haw?' I was thrilled that Brian had come.

The trial was on the top floor. I raced up the stairs and took up my position in the dock. The back of the room filled up with supporters. I was very moved that so many people had come to support me. It made a huge difference to feel that there were people in the room who were on my side and willing me on.

We all stood up as the District Judge, Caroline Tubbs, came in. When she'd sat down, we all sat down, and the proceedings started. I identified myself, and there was a short introduction by the clerk, then the prosecution presented its case. They produced two police officers, one of them Mil's arresting officer, Graham Wood, who spoke briefly. Then came the main prosecution witness, my arresting officer, PC Paul McInally, who read from his notebook. I was given a copy of it, as part of the evidence against me, so I can quote him exactly:

> I am currently attached to the Events and Operations office at Charing Cross Police Station as an Events planner. Part of this role involves processing applications for demonstrations within the designated area of Parliament under the Serious Organised Crime and Police Act 2005. I was made aware by PC281CX Scott that a male by the name of Milan Rai intended to hold an unauthorized demonstration at Richmond Terrace, Whitehall, SW1, opposite the gates of Downing Street.
>
> I checked the internet website www.indymedia.org and saw that a group known as Justice Not Vengeance were to hold an unauthorized protest opposite Downing Street. They intended to read out the names of the victims of the war in Iraq. This was to be on Tuesday 25 October 2005 starting at 0900 until 1300. I was assigned by the duty office to police this event.
>
> On Tuesday 25 October 2005 I was on duty in full uniform when I attended a briefing at Charing Cross Police Station at 0800. At the briefing the officers were split into two groups, and I was assigned as driver to an unmarked minibus. At 0900 we arrived at Richmond Terrace. I parked the vehicle in the centre of the road South of the women's war memorial facing south. The other minibus parked, again in the centre of the road facing North, just south of the entrance to Downing Street at Whitehall junction with Richmond Terrace. A barrier pen had been set out.

I saw two males standing outside the barrier pen at the start of the footway which leads to the Embankment. I saw PC Shannon leave the minibus with PC Goodwin to talk with the two males, one was IC1 [a white person] green/blue jacket [this was Cedric] the other was IC4 wearing a plastic rain coat. The two males walked off North of Whitehall at 09.25.

The IC4 [Asian] male, who I now know to be Milan Rai aged 40 years returned to the barrier pen area accompanied by a female who I now know to be Maya Anne Evans, 25 years, black hair, dark clothing. They were both carrying large pieces of cardboard. Approximately 15 feet behind them was a female who appeared to be videoing Mr Rai and Miss Evans as they appeared at the pen. They both entered the barrier pen and went to where there was a gap between the barriers. The female with the video camera crossed over to the Downing Street side and continued to video the pair.

Myself and PC Wood, PC Pratt left our vehicle and approached Mr Rai and Miss Evans. They had positioned the cardboard in front of the road, there was a large piece of white paper attached to each at the top of the one by Miss Evans in black type was 'www.j-n-v.org 100,000 Rings for Iraq'. The internet address I now know to be for Justice not Vengeance. Around her neck Miss Evans had an A4-sized placard. In her hand she had A4 sheets of paper titled 'British Military Deaths in Iraq'.

PC Wood went over to Mr Rai. I spoke to Miss Evans. I said to Miss Evans: 'Are you aware that this demonstration isn't authorised'. Miss Evans read out a name of a Fusilier from her sheet. I showed her a notice which explained about unauthorised demonstrations and offences under section 132 of the Serious Organized Crime and Police Act. I then said: 'I'll give you ten minutes to leave or you'll be arrested'. The time was 09.30am. Miss Evans continued to read out names looking towards Downing Street as she did so.

Two males went on to the road to photograph Miss Evans and Mr Rai. I went to the minibus and drove it over to the barrier pen.

At 09.42 I went back to Miss Evans and said: 'I am arresting you for taking part in an unauthorised demonstration in the designated area under section 132 of the Serious Organized Crime and Police Act 2005', and cautioned her. She made no reply. PC Wood arrested Mr Rai, they were both placed in the vehicle and escorted by PC Pratt and PC Wood.

After reading all this out, PC McInally was asked to read out the statement I'd made when I was charged, just before I was released from the police station:

> 'Today I took part in a remembrance ceremony to mark the deaths of 97 UK soldiers and an estimated 100,000 Iraqis. I believe that the war was illegal, and illegitimate, and troops should be withdrawn immediately.'

Behind me, I could hear lots of people murmuring agreement—and Brian Haw going: 'Yes!'

Then it was the turn of the defence. I left the dock and went into the witness box to gave my evidence. The usher asked me whether I wanted to swear an oath, or 'affirm'. 'Swearing' means using a sacred text, such as the Bible or the *Qur'an*. When you 'affirm', you promise to tell the truth, but without using a religious text. I said that I would affirm. A piece of paper was held out in front of me and I read it aloud: 'I do solemnly, sincerely and truly declare and affirm that the evidence I shall give shall be the truth, the whole truth and nothing but the truth.'

My barrister Alisdair then asked me questions in a calm, reassuring way. I focused on Alisdair and the judge. It was as if the other people in the courtroom faded away. I knew what the questions were going to be, I'd prepared my answers thoroughly and honestly, and I was confident about what I had to say. I forgot my nerves, just concentrating on what I had to do.

Alisdair began his questioning: 'Why were you demonstrating on the day of your arrest?'

I replied: 'I was taking part in an international anti-war campaign called 100,000 Rings for Iraq. The campaign was created to remember those who have died in the war with Iraq, and create awareness of the increasing mortality rate in Iraq. The campaign was set to run in the last week of

October as it marked the one year anniversary of the *Lancet* report, an article in a medical journal which estimated that 100,000 Iraqis had died since March 2003 as a direct result of the war. The campaign involved reading the names of 1,000 Iraqis while ringing a bell. The aim was to get 100 groups involved to make up 100,000. A name was to be read every minute over a period of 16 hours 40 minutes. We at JNV decided to split the long stint up into four blocks each lasting 4 hours 10 minutes. We also decided to include the list of British soldiers as victims of war. At the time of my arrest the figure stood at 97 British soldiers.'

Alisdair: 'So you had carried out the same demonstration at other locations?'

I said: 'Yes, the day before we had carried out the same demonstration outside Northwood Military Barracks. Northwood is the nerve centre for the operations in Iraq. Four days before then we carried out the same ceremony in Brighton outside the peace garden.'

Alistair: 'And were those occasions peaceful?'

I replied: 'Both events went peacefully. While at Northwood we were asked by a police officer to move across the road from the entrance of the military barracks as we were on MOD land. We co-operated with the request and were allowed to continue with the ceremony.'

Alisdair: 'What happened on the day of your arrest? Talk us through what you can remember.'

I said: 'Milan and I approached Whitehall on the morning of Tuesday 25 October. We set up our demonstration which consisted two A1 placards and some smaller chest signs. We also had leaflets to hand out inviting others to join our remembrance ceremony. We set up our placards over the barricades in front of the Cenotaph. We proceeded to start reading out the names of the dead. Milan started with the names of Iraqis then at intervals of 30 seconds I read a name of a British soldier. After the first few names I was approached by a police officer who informed me that I was demonstrating in a restricted protest zone without permission. I was informed that unless I moved on I would be arrested. I knew that I was in breach of this Act but decided to carry on. After a few minutes I was arrested and taken to Charing Cross Police station.'

Alisdair: 'And what was your behaviour like?'

I said: 'I was entirely peaceful and co-operative throughout the whole experience. I didn't resist arrest and went along with the requests of police officers.'

Then Alisdair asked: 'Why was it important for you to take part in the demonstration?'

I told the court: 'As a peace campaigner I feel very passionate about doing all I can to promote peace in Iraq. According to the *Lancet* estimate, the total number of people who've died in Iraq as a result of the invasion and occupation is over 100,000. I wanted to mark this loss of life and do what I could to publicise it. We were also heading towards the anniversary of the Fallujah massacre. Of the 700 bodies recovered from the rubble in Fallujah, 550 were women and children. 40 per cent of the buildings in the city were completely destroyed. Hospitals were targeted. It has now been admitted by the American forces that a terrifying chemical weapon, white phosphorus, was used in the attack. I think Iraq mortality is of great concern to both myself and the wider public.'

Alisdair: 'Why did you not seek permission?'

I said: 'I decided not to co-operate with this new piece of legislation as it is incompatible with the European Convention on Human Rights, Articles 10 and 11, freedom of expression and freedom of peaceful association with others. When thinking about seeking permission Milan and I were concerned that to co-operate with this piece of legislation was to co-operate with an erosion of our civil liberties in this country. We discussed the issues. Milan decided that he was not willing to comply with the legislation. I supported him in his decision as organizer, and told him I was willing to participate in an unauthorized demonstration. The Act gives the Metropolitan Police Commissioner the right to restrict the number of people at your demonstration, the period and the time, and I disagree with it. I didn't want to be arrested but, as far as I was concerned, I didn't think I was doing anything wrong standing there on a drizzly Tuesday morning with a colleague reading names of people who had died in a war. If anything, you could say it was similar to a Sunday remembrance service or even a funeral. I don't think it's a criminal offence and I don't think I should have been arrested for it. The person who decided on and supports the war in Iraq is Tony Blair and he lives in Downing Street—that's why we deliberately chose that location.'

Alisdair asked: 'Were the police aware that you were planning to carry out this demonstration?'

I said: 'The organizer of the demonstration Milan Rai took the initial steps of seeking permission from the police. He placed a phone call some weeks beforehand to the police informing them of our intentions. He followed this up with an email informing the police when and where we would be arriving, and told them that we would probably be no more than five in number. He was then told about the requirements of the Serious Organized Crime and Police Act 2005 which involved filling out an application form and asking for permission in order to hold our ceremony. He then refused to fill in this application form, and to ask for permission. But, yes, the police were fully aware of our intentions. We had informed them every step of the way.'

Then the Crown Prosecution Service lawyer stood up.

He asked: 'On the day of your arrest were you aware that you were in breach of the Serious Organised Crime and Police Act?'

I said: 'I was aware that I wasn't complying with the law'.

He asked: 'Why did you not ask for permission?'

I said: 'I don't see why I have to ask for permission to remember the dead.'

Naming The Dead

He said: 'So you knew you were breaking the law?'

I said: 'Yes, I knew that I was breaking the law'.

That was the end of questions from the prosecution. While I was answering the lawyers' questions, I saw the magistrate looking down at her desk. I could see she knew that what I was saying was true and sad, but that she didn't want to look me in the eye. I may be wrong, but I felt at the time that she was touched by my testimony.

Gabriel pointed out to me afterwards that instead of answering 'I knew I was breaking the law' in that last exchange, I should've said: 'I knew I was in breach of the Serious Organised Crime and Police Act', which is a slightly different thing. Our argument was that SOCPA was wrong, and therefore I wasn't 'breaking the law' when I participated in an unauthorized event. I wasn't denouncing the whole legal system, I was only refusing to co-operate with one particular part of it which was not valid.

Then Mil was called in to give his evidence as a witness. He had been waiting outside the court up until this point, so that his evidence to the court would not be affected by what other people had said. While outside, he'd been chatting to our arresting officers, who he was friendly with.

When Mil arrived in the witness box, he'd forgotten quite a few of the details he was asked about. He'd been travelling all night from Amsterdam, and he couldn't remember *when* he'd phoned up the Charing Cross Events Office notifying them of our event, or *who* he'd spoken to. I have to admit I found this vagueness funny at the time.

Apart from those minor details, his testimony sounded strong and reasonable and credible, and his explanation for what he'd done came across as well-thought-out. One odd thing about his appearance at my trial was that Mil still hadn't been charged with organizing the demonstration, while I was on trial for participating in it. By giving evidence, Mil added to the case against himself, by freely admitting in court that he had refused to co-operate with the new law.

After the defence case finished, we moved to legal arguments by both sides. Our argument was based on two articles from the European Convention on Human Rights. Article 10 says: 'Everyone has the right to freedom of expression.' Article 11 says: 'Everyone has the right to freedom of peaceful assembly'. Alisdair argued that section 132 of SOCPA, which laid new restrictions on protests near Parliament, was in conflict with these rights.

Unfortunately for us, magistrates' courts are not allowed to say that a law passed in Parliament is wrong. That can only be done by higher level courts. What Alisdair argued, however, was that District Judge Tubbs could 'read' section 132 in a special way, so that it became compatible with human rights law, which would have the effect that I should be acquitted of committing any crime.

Alisdair finished by stressing that the demonstration was peaceful and orderly, that I had expressed my views in a 'reasonable and measured' way, and that the police knew exactly what was going to happen. He ended: 'The defendant therefore submits that in all the circumstances she should be acquitted.'

The prosecution, of course, argued that there was no problem with the law, and that I should be convicted.

We then broke for lunch. Outside, Brian Haw spoke up in his usual passionate, poetic way: 'It was amazing! You came onto the stand and you were like an angel, and Milan came on and he was like an angel. Oh, the choreography was pure drama! Drama!'

I spent the lunch hour being interviewed, including a live interview with ITN. One woman from Radio 4 interviewed me before the trial started, at lunchtime, *and* after the trial. Emily had also done some media training with me. We thought about soundbites for different media— for the BBC, for the *Daily Mail*, and so on. The tabloids would probably want more about the British soldiers in Iraq whose names I'd been reading out when I was arrested. The BBC would probably want to hear about the

Naming The Dead

law itself. It was really useful preparing in detail, but when it came to the day itself, I just blurted all the soundbites out to everyone. But the training had helped me think about what journalists wanted to hear from me, so that I had the best chance of getting my point across.

After lunch, we went back into court. We stood up, the judge came in and sat down, and we all sat down again. Judge Tubbs told us that she had reached a verdict. She explained that magistrates' courts could not challenge laws passed by Parliament. Only the High Court could do that. I was obviously in breach of the Serious Organized Crime and Police Act, and therefore… she found me 'guilty'.

The judge turned immediately to the question of the fine. The prosecution asked for court costs of £400. After some discussion, Judge Tubbs decided that I should pay £100 in court costs, and £200 as a fine. Alisdair turned to me and asked me in a whisper: 'How much do you earn?'

I whispered back: 'I'm not going to pay!'

He said: 'Just tell me what your income is.'

I told him it was: 'Usually about £95 per week.'

He carried on whispering: 'How much could you pay off a week if you were paying?'

'£5 a week?' I offered reluctantly.

Alisdair turned to the judge and explained all these circumstances. The judge gave me 28 days to make the first payment. I haven't paid a penny, and I don't intend to.

If I'm completely honest, a small part of me had secretly hoped that there would be a miracle and we would win an acquittal. But really the verdict was not a surprise, it was what I'd expected from the moment I was arrested.

What I had not expected at all was the level of media interest. As soon as the judge left the court (we all stood up again), seven or eight journalists were on top of me, asking: 'And what do you think about the result?' 'How do you feel about the result?' 'What's your reaction to the judge's decision?' Reporters for the wire services, Associated Press and Reuters, were phoning in the story on their mobile phones. And all this was happening inside the court-room itself! I hadn't even got out of the defendants' box and I was being besieged.

Emily had helped me to prepare for the media during the trial, but I hadn't actually thought about what to say after the verdict, after the trial was over. I hadn't thought of any soundbites in advance.

Outside the building, there were more journalists. As I stepped out, it was like getting married, the part where you step outside the church and lots of people are taking your photograph. It was very intense. Because I'd done so much preparation, I stayed quite calm. I was pleased that I'd given the most that I could. I'd put a lot of energy into presenting a strong case and being as strong as I could.

I spent at least half an hour outside the court doing interviews with the press. It wasn't hugely mad outside the court, but it was constant. In the last interviews I gave, I was finding it really hard to string two sentences together, and I was getting really uptight. Brian Haw came up to me and said: 'Take a deep breath. Don't worry, you'll be fine. Just take a deep breath.' I took a few really deep breaths and then I carried on.

I really hadn't expected this level of press attention at all. We had put out a press release and I did think it would get picked up, but probably only by the London newspapers, not the nationals—and maybe the *Hastings Observer*. Finally it was all over, everyone had got what they wanted, and I could go home. Mil and I walked to Charing Cross station.

Travelling back to Hastings on the train, Mil turned to me and said: 'You do realize, in this afternoon alone you've experienced more media interest than I have in my whole twenty-year career as an activist.' We both laughed.

I was exhausted and I badly needed sleep. When I got home, I left my bag in the kitchen, went straight to my bedroom and fell asleep. It was 8pm. One of my last thoughts was: 'Thank God it's over.'

Chapter 11

Facing The World

8 December 2005

The morning after the trial, I decided to have a bath before work. It was about 8am, and I was lying in the bath when I heard my phone ringing. I thought: 'Ah, there may be some follow-up. Maybe one or two journalists want to check a few points with me.' My landlady Judy, who lives downstairs, knocked on the bathroom door and said: 'Er, Maya, it's the BBC on the phone for you. They want to interview you.' I jumped out of the bath, panicking. The BBC wanted me on the Vanessa Feltz show in half an hour. The researcher told me that my case was a big story, and on the front pages of several newspapers. I checked my mobile and I had 11 missed calls. It was 8.30 in the morning. I had never had 11 missed calls in my life! I was beginning to feel overwhelmed.

Every time I tried to check a message, another journalist rang, and I had to break off listening to the voicemail to talk to them. As I was speaking to one journalist, another would phone through. I'd put one on hold and say to the other, 'Yes, yes, yes.' They all wanted me to talk through what happened on the day of the arrest, and they all expressed shock that it had taken 14 police officers and a police van to arrest me. I made a timetable of interviews. Four radio interviews, three of them live, and one TV interview over the phone for the Steve Wright show.

Journalists rang saying they really wanted to interview me in person, and I'd say: 'Well, I'm kind of at work today.' It didn't occur to me to take the day off. I'd say: 'Maybe you can come to work and do the interview there?' So newspaper reporters and television cameras were all going to come in to Trinity Wholefoods. I rang work to tell them what was going on. Seth answered and I said: 'Seth, there's been this media coverage and it's been really huge and I'm going to be late for work. I'm really sorry.' He said: 'That's okay.' He paused, and then said: 'You do realize you're on the front page of the *Independent*?'

Journalists were calling me and doing interviews as I walked into work. When I saw the front of the *Independent*, I just went: 'Holy cow.' The front page featured the photographs of three people: myself, Flight Lieutenant Malcolm Kendall-Smith, 37, facing a court martial for refusing to fight in Iraq, and Douglas Barker, 72, threatened with jail for a tax protest against the Iraq war. The ironic headline was: 'War Criminals'. In the *Daily Mail*, the front page headline was: 'The land of free speech?' Both newspapers carried the same quote from me on the front page: 'I just think it's a shame you can't voice your freedom of speech in this country any more and it is illegal to hold a remembrance ceremony for the dead.'

When I got to work, there were journalists and photographers waiting outside. All day long, I was constantly doing interviews. A few weeks earlier, I'd been reluctant to be the first SOCPA defendant on trial. I'd wanted to avoid being the centre of attention. I'd forced myself to be strong, and make the best case that I could. But I'd assumed that it would just for be for that day, being on trial and then doing some presswork on the day. It had never even crossed my mind that it would go on any longer than that. But, to my surprise, I found that once I was in the middle of the storm of media attention, I just had to get on with it. Then I found I was really enjoying it, and I wasn't afraid of doing it any more. I felt I was doing it well.

The media attention didn't stay at that level, of course. But I continued to get phone calls from journalists, especially to comment on free speech and the right to protest over the next few months. At the end of January, I was asked to come on BBC Newsnight to debate with Jeremy Paxman and a government minister.

Sort of by accident, I'd actually been prepared for this challenge by my friends a few days earlier, when I was invited to a 'Seeds of Hope Ploughshares' celebration at the home of Andrea Needham, who lives in Hastings. As I explained earlier, Andrea was one of the four women who were found 'not guilty' of criminal damage after they hammered on a British Aerospace warplane that was about to be exported to Indonesia (and which would then have been used on people in East Timor). The 'Seeds of Hope Ploughshares' women argued in court that the damage was legal, given Indonesia's record in East Timor and the criminal use that the Hawk jet would be put to if exported. The jury agreed with them and they were found 'not guilty'.

There were just a few other people there, including Mil and Gabriel Carlyle, coordinator of Voices in the Wilderness UK. First Andrea and Emily talked about the action, (Emily was in the support group). I hadn't known the details before, and I was amazed at the amount of work they put into the action, and then into the court case. I felt quite emotional hearing their story. People who I knew had done something so amazing. I was moved and inspired.

During the evening, we watched videos about the action, including one of Andrea appearing on Newsnight. I thought: 'Wow, she's been on Newsnight! That's amazing; that I know someone who's been on Newsnight!' I thought she was brilliant. Gabriel said that Andrea should have interrupted more, but she explained that she couldn't, because she wasn't in the studio, she was being beamed in by satellite from a box in a BBC studio in Liverpool.

So when I was invited onto Newsnight, I felt strengthened by Andrea's strong performance, and I remembered

Gabriel's words about interrupting. Here is the transcript of part of that Newsnight discussion:

Jeremy Paxman: Were the police at all embarrassed when they arrested you?

Maya: Not immediately no, I don't think so. My arresting officer justified the piece of legislation by saying it actually helped the police with their organization of protests within the restricted protest zone. And that in fact I had been arrested that day for my own safety, as there may have been more than one demonstration taking place on that day and those two demonstrations may have come into conflict.

Paxman: (Turning to Home Office minister John Denham) What sort of society are we living in when a woman like this who doesn't look to me to be a big threat to anyone is arrested by police for a peaceful protest?

John Denham: We've just seen on the TV today a peaceful protest taking place in Parliament Square today. So there's no ban on protest in Parliament Square. What the legislation says, if you want to have a protest, you get police authorisation. Now Jeremy, twenty years ago I organised a protest against third world debt, right at the door of Downing Street. I actually went and organised that with the police beforehand. I didn't have to by law.

Paxman: What sort of society are we living in where you have to have police permission to demonstrate?

Denham: Because actually the convention which says how we use our rights to protest have broken down and that is why parliament has introduced some limited restrictions for reasons of security and protection of the way our democracy works.

Maya: Can I just interject here?

Paxman: Go on.

Maya: With my protest, in fact we had informed the police a week beforehand and when we arrived they were expecting us and they knew the group we were from: Justice not Vengeance. Today I attended a spontaneous protest which was organized for the day the 100th [British] soldier in Iraq was killed and therefore, as far as I know an application for that protest did not occur. So in fact that protest was illegal.

Denham: The protest we just saw was authorized... We have to accept, Jeremy, that one of the things which have changed over the last 20 years from the time when my job was organizing protests, which it was for a number of organizations, is that there were restraints on what you did, many of those have broken down. Pressure groups now have no compunction about breaking into parliament, about throwing things at the Prime Minister.

Paxman: She wasn't doing that! She was reading the list of British soldiers who have perished in Iraq!

Denham: Nobody wants to stop that, and I wouldn't.

Paxman: But she *was* stopped!

Denham: The reason...

Paxman: She was arrested for doing it.

Denham: The reason why Parliament has legislated is that over the past few years other protest groups, the Countryside Alliance and others have shown themselves willing to disrupt the way things operate. I regret the need to pass that legislation. But the truth is, it has come in response to certain groups who have tried to disrupt the way in which Parliament wants to operate. I think that somebody like Maya ought to be able to stand up....

Paxman: But she's not!

Denham: ....and do that demonstration.

Paxman: She got prosecuted for it!

To everyone's surprise, my case briefly became the centre of political debate in Britain. I think it gave people the opportunity to express their anger at the erosion of freedom under New Labour, as well their sadness at the ongoing war in Iraq.

Roy Hattersley, the former Deputy Leader of the Labour Party, called SOCPA 'indefensible'. He wrote: 'To require every demonstration within shouting distance of Parliament to obtain permission from the police is in direct contradiction of the principles which should govern a free society. Miss Evans has done the nation a service by demonstrating how ridiculous the law has become. The Government should reciprocate by repealing it.'

A few days later, there was an exchange about the case on the BBC Radio 4 Today programme, between Lord Falconer, the Secretary of State for Constitutional Affairs, and presenter John Humphrys. John Humphrys asked:

'Can I turn to another subject, fairly quickly, and that is freedom of speech. What's happened to it? Why have we lost it? Why can't a woman stand near Number 10 Downing Street and read out a list of names without being arrested?'

Lord Falconer responded: 'Freedom of speech is alive and well in this country'. John Humphrys jumped in: 'So long as you don't exercise it near Parliament!' Which led to this exchange:

Lord Falconer: Don't be ridiculous!
Humphrys: I'm not being ridiculous!
Falconer: You are. We are a country which couldn't be freer, in its press, in what people say –
Humphrys: So long as you don't want to exercise it near Parliament within one kilometre.
Falconer: The idea that you take a measure which is a public order measure, designed to protect our Parliament building as depriving people of freedom of speech is ridiculously overdone, if I may say so.
Humphrys: I shall bear that in mind next time I want to stand outside Parliament and read my newspaper aloud, possibly an editorial that somebody doesn't like.

You may not believe this, but in June 2006, someone was actually stopped and questioned by the police for holding a newspaper outside Downing Street! It was a copy of the *Independent* with a front-page headline saying: 'Warning: if you read this newspaper you may be arrested under the Government's anti-terror laws'.

Naming The Dead

Chapter 12

Our Power

Make That Change

A few days after my trial, my local MP in Hastings Michael Foster (who thinks that a large part of terrorism comes from 'evil people') wrote to the *Independent* to attack me. He argued that 'with the current terrorist threat it would be easy to mask a terrorist atrocity under the guise of a legitimate demonstration'. He suggested that if only I had notified the police in advance, as Mil did, then I would not have been tried, just as Mil, up to that date, had not been tried. Of course a month later Mil *was* charged. Eventually he was convicted, and fined £350. Mr Foster ignored the fact I was a 'participant' in the demonstration, with no need to notify the police I was attending the ceremony.

SOCPA does not 'ban' demonstrations, but my MP had failed to understand the real problems.

Mr Foster (who is a lawyer) had completely misunderstood the difference between 'notifying' the police (which we did, and were happy to do) and 'applying for authorization' (which we refused to do). We had no problem with letting the police know when our demonstration was planned to take place, to make sure that we weren't going to clash with another demonstration by someone else. We were not prepared to ask the permission of the police, and to give them the opportunity to impose arbitrary restrictions on our remembrance ceremony.

And as for Mr Foster's idea that terrorists will be stopped by SOCPA: a piece of paper from Charing Cross police station is not going to stop anyone turning up to a political protest with a gun or a bomb, if that's what they are determined to do.

A few days after Mr Foster's letter, the *Independent* received a suitable response from Major Frank Baldwin, a Royal British Legion Volunteer in London:

> As an ex-soldier I was incensed by Michael Foster MP's argument that the arrest of Maya Evans under the Serious Organised Crime and Police Act is for our protection. Why should political protests be more of a cover for terrorist attacks on the Houses of Parliament than the tourists or commuters who were the most recent cover for terrorism? Miss Evans' criminal act was to read the names of our war dead at the Cenotaph, our national war memorial. The Royal British Legion's exhortation is a promise to remember those who have given their lives for their country. How can someone reading out the names of our war dead ever be a criminal offence? If remembering our dead has become a crime, then it can only be because Mr Foster and his government have a guilty conscience about their deaths.

Since my trial, I've had a lot of letters of support from people who feel exactly the same way. I don't think I've had a single hostile letter (though I have received one hostile email). I'm very grateful for all the support that people have expressed to me, which I really appreciate.

I think people have been touched by the fact that I was reading the names of the dead, particularly as I happened to be reading the names of the British war dead (while Mil read the Iraqi names). The spirit of remembrance was part of our action, and I think people responded to that.

I think also that because Mil wasn't charged until a month after my trial, and I was tried on my own, people had the impression that I did the action by myself, or that I had masterminded it. In Hastings, people started coming in and saying: 'Oh, you've got a double life! I saw you on TV the other day.' People started talking about politics to me. In fact, it became quite difficult working at Trinity sometimes. Virtually all the customers were supportive, which I really appreciated, but doing my work and engaging with people intensely all the time could be quite a strain at times.

I had a problem with just one customer who seemed to assume that we were both white and Christian, and that we'd both be hostile to Islam. I made a point, a few weeks later, of introducing him to my schoolfriends, Rania and Adesina, who were both wearing headscarves. I'm partly from an ethnic minority background, I've been brought up with ethnic minorities, and I have a deep respect for Islam and for the Muslim community.

I know that there are people who are suspicious of Islam as a religion, and who think that it is more violent than other religions. I just don't see this. All religions are manipulated to fit the agendas of particular individuals and groups. If you look back to the teachings of the Prophet Muhammad, he said it was *haram* (sinful) to wage war except in self-defence—just like most Christians, I think.

Yes, Islam needs, and is going through, a religious modernisation, just as Christianity is still going through reforms in relation to the marriage of same-sex couples, female priests, and so on. In many places, Muslim women are standing up against the oppressive measures used against them in the name of Islam. They are working *within* Islam to change things. However this process can't get anywhere if Muslim countries continued to be threatened and attacked.

Real change, whether social or personal, takes time. I've experienced in my own life how someone can gradually develop their own opinions, and slowly become more confident in expressing them, until they are willing to cross the line of what the government considers legality.

As I've described in this book, I began my adult life as a quiet, quite withdrawn person, who then became an ordinary party-going young woman for several years. It was the shock of the 'war on terror', and the aggressive wars against Afghanistan and Iraq, that really started the change.

With the support and companionship of my friends in Merseyside Stop The War, I began becoming an activist. Through the inspiration I gained through working with the wonderful people of Voices in the Wilderness US, I was fired up to really change direction in my life. In Hastings, I've developed so much as a person and an activist through working alongside my friends in Hastings Against War and Justice Not Vengeance. Then it was the special community feeling we created on the Hiroshima Peacewalk in the summer of 2005 that empowered me and encouraged me to experiment with 'crossing the line'. It was all a long process of personal change with lots of support and inspiration from other people which helped me get to the point where I knew how I felt about the war in Iraq and about the erosion of freedom in Britain, and I became determined to act on how I felt.

I feel strongly about how our freedoms are being eroded, for example by the proposed National Identity Card and National Identity Register. I don't think it's only the guilty who have to fear a massive state database containing private information about each and every one of us. That kind of information can be misused by the government, and collecting it all into one place makes it easier for identity thieves and other unauthorized people to gain access to health, police and credit records and so on. After learning a lot about identity cards, I decided that I would refuse to carry one, and I joined the No2ID campaign.

At the same time, while I feel strongly about what is going on in the world, I also believe strongly in nonviolence. Nonviolence, to me, means not harming other living things. I don't think you can be 'violent' towards property, and I think in certain circumstances it can be justified to damage property. For example, the Seeds of Hope Ploughshares action in 1996 caused property damage, but it was morally justified, and it was found to be legally justified.

I know that most people tend to think that violence can be justified in certain circumstances, but I'm dubious. Violence gets things done quickly, but if you start off with violence, it seems to me that it's very difficult to move away from violence. If there's a violent revolution and you have a new social structure that's been brought about by violence, I think it's hard to see how you won't be tempted to stick to violence to keep it in place. Although things don't move as quickly through nonviolence, I think it's worth it in the long run.

Civil disobedience means being willing to be arrested—seen as 'breaking the law'—to highlight an issue in a vivid fashion. Civil disobedience isn't always justified. I think it's justified when a terrible harm is being done—or is about to be done—and the 'normal' channels of lobbying and letter-writing and demonstrating aren't working.

Having said that, I didn't rush into civil disobedience, and I wouldn't recommend anyone else rushing into it. For example, I went to a nonviolent direct action (NVDA) training session long before I ever took part in an arrestable action. After the 'Airbourne' demonstration in Eastbourne in 2004 I talked about earlier, I went to an NVDA workshop in Hastings organised by 'Seeds for Change'. We did some practical work in terms of what to do when you get arrested, and there was a legal briefing. The whole session was about two hours long. When you know more about what you're doing, you feel more motivated to be involved. It is much more frightening walking into something that you don't know much about. After the workshop, I felt more confident that I had the skills to conduct myself in a way that would be more penetrating to the police and passers-by. I learnt how to conduct myself in a situation of civil disobedience. Then, of course, I went on a one-day training when I was on the Hiroshima Peacewalk.

If you get involved in civil disobedience without going to a training, I think you can get yourself into a situation you didn't really want to be in, and then afterwards feel pretty bitter about it all. Instead of feeling empowered and being the most effective you could have been, you might feel as if you haven't achieved anything, and that it was an emotionally draining experience for nothing.

One of the hardest things to cope with as a peace activist is the slow pace of change. I saw depression and despondency set in after the invasion of Iraq, for example. People often tell me that what I am doing is pointless and will achieve nothing. If the march on 15 February 2003 couldn't stop the war…

Personally, I gain strength from the examples of change we see in history. For example, the change we have seen recently with animal rights. Before the 1960s, very few people in the West were vegetarian or considered the fact that animals have feelings. Now, although the poor treatment of animals has probably become more extreme with battery farming, animal testing, and so on, there has been a major shift in our attitudes towards animals. Fox hunting has been outlawed. Vegetarian options are usually available on a menu, and laws exist to safeguard the treatment of animals in commercial farming. The number of vegetarians in Britain is thought to have increased from 100,000 in 1945 to nearly 4 million today, while the number of vegans has more than doubled in the past decade to around 250,000.

Although the situation is far from ideal, our awareness of animal suffering has improved considerably. Working in a wholefood shop I saw changes in people's understanding and behaviour happening all the time.

Being in the peace movement has helped me to appreciate that change is born out of lots of small drops in the ocean. Expecting change overnight can be emotionally suicidal. At the same time, sometimes we have a dramatic effect way beyond what we were expecting. I suppose our remembrance ceremony is an example of that.

Another much more powerful example comes from the Vietnam War. It's in Mil's book, *War Plan Iraq*, and we put it into the JNV documentary *Counter Terror: Build Justice*. What I find amazing is that the big Vietnam Moratorium demonstration, which happened in Washington DC on 15 October 1969, where 100,000 people were calling for an end to the war, had an effect completely unknown to the organizers.

Secretly, President Nixon had issued a series of nuclear threats against North Vietnam amounting to a nuclear ultimatum. Nixon was trying to force the North Vietnamese government to effectively surrender, and to force the South Vietnamese guerrillas to halt their war on US forces, and he was threatening to drop a nuclear bomb on North Vietnam if this did not happen by 1 November 1969.

After the Vietnam Moratorium demonstration, the President's advisers told him that he could not use the nuclear bomb, because it would obviously cause such a huge wave of protest—'internal physical turmoil'. As Mil put it in his book, 'mobilized public opinion averted the world's second nuclear war'. And the demonstrators had no idea of what they had accomplished.

We have power, more power than we know. By being active with our friends and neighbours, by educating the people we live and work with, and by putting pressure on those who make crucial decisions, we do change the world. Not as fast as we'd like to, but we do.

I hope that my story will encourage more people to become active for whatever cause is close to their hearts. I hope especially that some people who read this, who oppose the ongoing war in Iraq, will be encouraged to support and become active with their local peace groups, so we will not have to keep remembering the deaths of an ever-increasing number of Iraqi civilians and Western soldiers.

Most of the time we will make painfully slow progress. Sometimes our actions will have an impact far beyond what we expect or can imagine.

Naming The Dead

On 25 October 2005, we only managed to read a few names before we were arrested:

Sergeant Chris Hickey, 30, died 18 October 2005
Captain Ken Masters, 40, died 15 October 2005
Major Matthew Bacon, 34, died 11 September 2005
Fusilier Donal Anthony Meade, 20, died 5 September 2005
Fusilier Stephen Robert Manning, 22, died 5 September 2005
Second Lieutenant Richard Shearer, 26, died 16 July 2005
Private Leon Spicer, 26, died 16 July 2005
Private Phillip Hewett, 21, died 16 July 2005
Signaller Paul William Didsbury, 18, died 29 June 2005
Lance Corporal Alan Brackenbury, 21, died 29 May 2005
Guardsman Anthony John Wakefield, 24, died 2 May 2005
Private Mark Dobson, 41, died 28 March 2005
Squadron Leader Patrick Marshall, 39, died 30 January 2005
Flight Lieutenant David Stead, 35, died 30 January 2005
Flight Lieutenant Andrew Smith, 25, died 30 January 2005

Heder Gwad Shrge Alarthe, 3, died 28 March 2003
Heder Mnam Mhmed Aljbore, 43, died 28 March 2003
Hse Rahe Hasan, 14, died 28 March 2003
Hsen Easer Mthlom, 33, died 28 March 2003
Hsen Gasem Swelaa Alkekane, 35, died 28 March 2003
Husaam Hameed Hanoon, 21, died 28 March 2003
Husien Khelaan Mutleq, 30, died 28 March 2003
Imad Hamed Abed Al-Ameer, age unknown, died 28 March 2003
Jaber Hasan Hawash, age unknown, died 28 March 2003
Jalial Abed Al-Zahraa, 21, died 28 March 2003
Jehaad Jaleel Ketrran, age unknown, died 28 March 2003
Jmela Hmed Lfta Alsaade, 24, died 28 March 2003
Jumaa Ghazi Aamer, 39, died 28 March 2003
Jwde Abas Aghode Algnabe, 28, died 28 March 2003
Kald Kswb Abas Alsaade, 30, died 28 March 2003

We invite all readers of this book to hold or participate in a ceremony of remembrance for those who have died in Iraq. Longer lists of names can be found via the Justice Not Vengeance website <www.j-n-v.org>.